How to Make People Do What You Want

Influence Human Behavior to Persuade People and Win Friends

Christopher Rothchester

Table of Contents

Introduction

Congratulations on purchasing How to Make People Do What You Want, and I thank you heartily for doing so.

Whenever I start reading a book and it begins with an introduction outlining everything in detail that I'm about to read about, I think: "Just let me find that out when I read it!" So I will spare you the burden of hearing some long description of what you are about to read. Suffice it to say that I prepared this book with care, with you in mind, your future, your happiness, and I earnestly hope that through these pages I can help you in some way. The following chapters will discuss how to overcome yourself to reach your full potential. In order to be a charismatic, pleasant, happy person, you may need to overcome some habits. When we change how we think, we change who we are, we become a new person. No, you don't need to forget who you are and lose your personality, you just need to control your own life rather than letting someone or something else rule you. None of us want to be slaves or be imprisoned, but how do you escape a prison or slavery that you don't know you're in? You can't! So you have to become aware of what is influencing your life and hindering your ability to accomplish your goals. To be truly free, limitless, powerful, and loving, you need to know yourself well. This book will show you how to understand how you think and how to relate to others. I truly hope this may propel you forward in the road of life.

There are plenty of books on this subject out there, and I honestly doubt that my humble skill has produced the best one by any means, but I do hope this may be a good start for you. Thanks again for choosing my little book! Now let's begin...

Chapter 1: Develop Balanced Self Confidence

How do you feel about yourself? Your answer to this question will affect how you deal with others and how you treat yourself. Some people think too much of themselves and others think too little; balance can be hard to find. I have experienced both at different times.

At first, quite a few years ago, I used to overestimate my abilities, but after failing to achieve my expectations a few times, I was put in my place. Then I began to underestimate myself, fearing failure around every corner. Eventually, I found that none of the things I feared ever seemed to happen, as I usually did better than I'd supposed.

The challenge is to reach a happy medium and have a moderate view of yourself. Not one of us is by any means insignificant, we all have our unique purpose to fulfill in life, and at the same time, not one of us is entitled to special respect, whatever rank you may belong to or aspire to. To think of ourselves properly, we must consider what makes someone "great."

Some people believe celebrities are great, but why? Mostly because they are paid well and are well-known by society, but how does that make them unique? It seems to me that most celebrities got where they are by means of either chance, friendly connections in their industry, or ruthlessly clawing their way to the top. None of these things makes them superior. Some celebrities, though not many, are truly admired for their kindness and compassion, using their high position and wealth to help others. You notice here that there is a difference between Greatness and Popularity.

The most revered and beloved people throughout history have been those who gave every last drop of their devotion to a noble cause or selflessly helping people. Think of Gandhi, Martin Luther King Jr., Robin Hood, Jesus of Nazareth, George Washington, Joan of Arc, and plenty more. Regardless of your opinions of such people, it is undeniable they are highly esteemed because of their unbreakable determination and service to others. If we aim to emulate their path and follow in their footsteps, we too cannot be selfish or even self-centered; we must be servants. We are to be servants, yes, but not slaves; free and sovereign, respectable, confident, and with purpose.

Mahatma Gandhi began his career being trained as a lawyer in London and subsequently moved to South Africa after a short period back in India. He supported the British in a war against the Boer minority despite his sympathizing with the Boers. He also supported the British Empire in World War I, believing India would gain independence after the war. When his hopes were disappointed, he began his satyagraha (nonviolent resistance) movement in earnest. This became his purpose in life, and he is well remembered for what he did thereafter. He simplified his life, living with less luxury than the average Indian peasant, which allowed him to focus on serving others.

Indeed, the key to being a servant to others and yet realizing our own significance is to find our personal purpose. Everybody has one, and there's no reason to even live at all without one. A purposeless person will inevitably be depressed and bored, perpetually sensing there is something missing in their lives. But even despite having a purpose, some become presumptuous, believing their wisdom to be of such great importance and scarcity that anybody lacking this wisdom is a fool. In order to avoid such a "high and mighty" attitude, we have to acknowledge our relative insignificance in the grand scheme of things. Yes, we each have a unique and important purpose, but if we fail to accomplish it, somebody else will; we are not likely divinely ordained prophets—so don't get "too big for your britches!"

But there's more to the story of self-confidence: the physical aspect. Now, unfortunately, this one is much more challenging because we can always change our minds, but only so much of our physical appearances can be changed. If we are not content and comfortable with our appearances, we will be sheepish and uncomfortable dealing with people. When I was younger, and my face mottled with blemishes, I was extremely embarrassed about my appearance and wished I could go off into the wilderness as a hermit and be seen by nobody. Eventually, I realized that if I had a confident way about how I carried myself, people seldom noticed my imperfections, or if they did, they didn't dwell on them too long.

Everybody has something to be thankful for in their looks. Now, I can't lie; some people are just plain ugly, or at least less showy than others. If you feel that you are in this category, ask yourself: "Am I being fair with myself or am I selling myself short." It may be that looks are really just not your strong suit, if so, consider focusing on just being a kindhearted person, having inner beauty (which is more important anyway), and likely, after getting to know you better, people will care less about how you look. But, why not do everything in your power to improve your looks? If you have some weight you'd like to lose, be determined to commit and live a more wholesome lifestyle to help you accomplish that goal. Living an active lifestyle, a diet low in sugar and carbohydrates, and being out in nature are sure to help. If you have a skin problem, say acne perhaps: go out in the sun, get a tan (which makes blemishes less noticeable), take cold showers (which close the pores and reduce inflammation), wash your face with baking soda, minimize your consumption of sugary processed foods, and exercise. It is a necessity that you find a way to content yourself with your appearance once you've done all you can to improve it, because your happiness will suffer otherwise.

Did your grandma ever tell you to "stand up straight and stop slouching"? If not, you've likely heard it somewhere else. Beyond the skeletal benefits of standing up straight, it also helps us feel at ease. Our body and mind are intricately connected: your mind affects the body and your body affects the mind. If you stand tall, relax your shoulders, puff out your chest, suck in your gut, raise your eyes high, and walk with a broad stride, you will feel more self-assured. Start good habits and they will change how you feel about yourself.

Once you are confident in your appearance and your purpose in life, you need to be confident in your ability to have intelligent conversations with people. If you believe that everybody is wiser than you, you will be shy, which is fine, but as I've found over the years, being uncomfortable around people is just plain unpleasant. It's much nicer to place no limits on yourself, be able to do anything, and be anywhere without feeling nervous.

Do you feel uptight around people? I know I sure did. I would get overpoweringly hot, start sweating, time would move unnaturally slow, and my eyes would even tear up. All that just from being in a crowd. Now I'm free of all those symptoms, except when I wear a woolen suit, I will get hot! Why? It takes work, but a good start is to realize this: what can people really do to you? The worst that could conceivably happen is for you to make an utter fool of yourself, and you might never see the person again anyway. If you do have to see them again, they'll understand, everybody makes mistakes. Nobody expects you to be perfect, except perhaps yourself. In which case, you need to get over perfectionism; do your best, whatever that may be, and ask for nothing more than that.

For a long time, I convinced myself that I enjoyed shyness, and was proud of it. If you want to be a "man of few words" then by all means do so, what you do say will be more highly respected when you say it and nobody will be able to criticize you for being a chatterbox. Nevertheless, I eventually realized that social timidity was simply fear, and nobody wants to be ruled by fear. If you want to be a hermit, be one! Just don't be afraid of what can't hurt you. Be quiet by choice, not by fear of making a fool of yourself.

For a long time when I used to be shy, people would always try and crack my shell, get me to talk. So they'd put me on the spot and pepper me with personal questions, which only made me feel more uncomfortable. But eventually, I realized that if I were to ask them a lot of questions (not being rude, just making conversation) to keep them on their toes, they'd oftentimes actually start looking around nervously and try to cut the conversation short. The reason for this unusual behavior is that dominant people like to dominate a conversation, and they enjoy speaking to children and shy people in general because they feel at ease with them and get the opportunity to dominate the conversation. It is seldom meant to be inconsiderate, certainly not malicious; they likely don't even realize they're doing it. But if you take advantage of a knowledge of how such people think, you can "give them their own medicine" and get the upper hand in what would usually be an awkward discussion. Understanding psychology at first makes one feel disgusted with people, believing everything they do is motivated by some subconscious primal impulse, but further knowledge permits one to have compassion for others, seeing as their intentions are pure. But we will discuss these subjects in more detail later on.

If you are downright horrified at the idea of having to ask outgoing, extroverted people questions, as was I, here are some suggestions to help. Try talking to yourself. Take a walk in the woods, the hills, the prairies, the beach, or some other isolated spot and have a full-blown conversation with yourself. If you are deliberating on a problem or coming to a decision on something, take both sides and debate the subject out loud. When you get accustomed to conversing naturally by yourself, it will also extend to real conversations with other people. To this day, I still go out in the backwoods and talk to the trees, sometimes speaking for them and other times letting the sound of the wind in their leaves do the answering. Strange perhaps to most people, I know, but beneficial for more than one reason. Another vital skill for mastering conversation is a robust vocabulary; so in order to build your word usage: read, read, and read; just like you're doing right now! Another thing to keep in mind is the physical side of things. If you feel good and have mental clarity, conversation will come easy, but if you feel sickly, bloated, and have brain fog, then you'd likely rather sit alone in the woods someplace. Remember, being a hermit is wonderful; I'd like to try it myself some time (at least till I start to miss people), but if social interaction is inescapable for you, then there's only one thing to do: learn to like it.

But what if you're already confident, perhaps too confident? If you come off to people as overbearing and domineering, they'll likely be put off by you. So how would you go about bringing your view of yourself back into balance? If you believe you are special, gifted, or skilled—you may well be right, but let's bring it into perspective. There will always be somebody who's better than you, no matter how skilled you may be. And even if you are exceptional and the best in the world at what you do, you can't be the best at everything! Everybody has their own strengths and weaknesses; learn to respect the strengths of others even if you don't understand them or would prefer your own skills. And not to scare you, but you do well to remember that your gifts could disappear in a blink of an eye, if some tragic accident befalls you and your skill could be snatched right out of your hands. Our skills are indeed gifts, so let's be grateful for them and likewise admire the gifts of others, neither disrespecting them nor envying them.

Another issue many folks encounter is the urge to compare themselves to others and judge themselves according to their observations. Each of us is an unfathomably complex, unmatchable, and singularly unique being with our own high purpose and beautiful, vast potential. Whether that potential is attained or not (as some people are born with disabilities or other encumbrances that hinder their ability to achieve their full potential), each of us is worthy of being assessed individually and not by somebody else's standard. If we do our very best and only that, and we constantly seek our continual betterment, we have nothing to be condemned for. Oftentimes, the standards that people set for themselves, they extend to all humanity, and if anybody doesn't measure up to their "right" level, that person or those people are deemed inferior. All cultures, societies, and even families and individuals are raised differently—it is not for us to judge.

At the same time, overconfidence in our abilities may lead to humiliation. I have noticed a few acquaintances who resolutely believed in their ability to accomplish something, namely throwing a football, but this overconfidence paralyzed and stunted their interest in practicing their skills. At the time, these friends of mine boasted of their athletic prowess, and so we proceeded to play a little game of football. The result was hilarious; upon flinging the ball, it turned over and over, not a bit of spin or arrow-like straightness to it, rather it veered off into the nearby woods. After such a spectacle, this individual attempted to excuse himself by a defense: his shoulder had been hurting, and he was off his game. And that may have been true, but he didn't see fit to mention that beforehand, which would have been more fitting than boasting. If perhaps this fellow, rather than talking up his skills, simply practiced his athletics, those who played with him might have been surprised and impressed, seeing fit to compliment him. It is better to be silent about our supposed skills, letting others compliment us instead, for if we ever cease to live up to our claims, we will be quite humbled.

Self-confidence also can have a cumulative effect on your performance in life. If you strongly believe in yourself, you are more likely to succeed in whatever your goal may be; and even if you fail, you learn from the mistake and try again with more experience. On the other hand, if from the very beginning you doubt your ability and have a negative attitude, your chances of success are lower, and failure will only reinforce that pessimistic attitude, so you will likely give up thereafter. This brings us to another subject: Optimism vs. Pessimism.

Some people believe it to be prudent to expect the worst and hope for the best so that if they fail, it will be no surprise, and if they succeed, it will be a pleasant and unexpected joy. The issue with that mentality is that it lessens your motivation to try and succeed because success seems a remote possibility not worth striving for. Instead, expect and strive for the best, and if such is not attained, then view the shortcoming as a lesson that will only enable you to do better next time. This idea is summed up in Mr. Thomas Edison's famous quote: "I never once failed. I just found 2,000 ways not to make a light bulb; I only needed to find one way to make it work." If we view every challenge not as a burden but as a lesson and gift to strengthen us and show us the way to our goals, then we will undoubtedly be quite content, at peace, and confident.

Our positive attitude about life should also apply to ourselves. As the saying goes: "we are our own worst critic." The average person finds it easy to excuse and forgive others for their little mistakes, but for themselves—it's quite another story. Such ones have compassion for others but very little left over for themselves. Don't be too hard on yourself; show yourself the same mercy you would show others.

At one of my old jobs, I worked at a family-run farm. My boss was an elderly grouch (but he was kind deep down though) and his daughter, let's call her Agatha, she was very self-deprecating. Her father excused no mistakes whatsoever and required everything to be done precisely his way, even if his workers found it easier, quicker, and more efficient to do it another way. Now Agatha, growing up in this environment, learned to be inordinately hard on herself so her father wouldn't. She prolonged this habit into adulthood. She certainly didn't treat people in the harsh way her father did, but she sure treated herself that way. If she forgot the slightest thing or made one trivial mistake, she would get worked up, calling herself a "[blank] idiot." This merciless attitude towards herself was undoubtedly unhealthy and resulted in constant disappointment and annoyance. Being from a more relaxed background myself, I was wholly unaccustomed to such an attitude about life. The people I meet in urbanized areas are like aggressive workhorses that push themselves and their companions bloody because they are in a rush all the time. Where I come from, people slow down and learn patience; they prioritize kindness and common sense over rigidity and rules. If more people could learn to live and think like country people, we'd have a happier and more confident world.

Your environment, even the weather can affect your attitude as well. Where I grew up, I'll tell you, no doubt about it; it was really hot! Blistering hot, in fact. Just step out the door, and you're already sweating bucketfuls, and after getting a few things done, you'd go inside and take about a half hour just to cool down and dry off. We tried to get our yard work done in the mornings and evenings when it was a little cooler, and the hard work like cutting, hauling, and burning dead trees we'd do come winter. Before I learned my lesson, I used to move, talk, and think a little faster and more intensely than I ought to have. I soon realized an important lesson for a hot climate: slow down or burn up. So I learned to talk slowly, move slowly and smoothly, and even think calmly and methodically. Getting impatient, frustrated, or agitated in any way, even a little bit, would cause my body to overheat. So I took the natural course of action: calm down. Ever since then, the heat bothers me less, and the cold bothers me more, but that's a story for another day. Not all of us had the good fortune to be born in the countryside, but we have got to learn those lessons to be at peace with the world and ourselves.

For the most part, we are our own worst critics, but sometimes, others can be. If we have to deal with verbally abusive and insulting people, and there is no reasonable way to escape associating with them, we need to learn a few things. First of all, remember that nobody's born a bully; something turns them mean. Perhaps they had an abusive parent or experienced trauma. Understanding this, we can hopefully find it in our hearts to pity them; really they're only hurting themselves—if they hurt you, it's because you let them. Oftentimes bullies simply feel insecure themselves, their own self-esteem is suffering. Deep down, they want to feel good about themselves, not feel worthless. So they may enviously attack you in order to get you to feel as bad as them. They may not think of it that way, likely they don't even know what they're doing. You need to develop a thick skin, just because they say something doesn't mean it's true. Try to learn to think logically, not emotionally; no, they haven't ruined your life, they're just trying to make it harder. The one who harms others harms himself, nobody else can harm us emotionally but ourselves. So don't let their taunts get to you; they are projecting their own problems onto you, just pity them— maybe even try to help them. When somebody is the hardest to love is when they need the most love. Try to kill them with kindness, and they likely won't be able to continue bothering you. If you give them some kindness (something they surely need whether they know it or not), not only will you help them but also yourself—it will boost your own confidence. You know, "what doesn't kill you makes you stronger."

Speaking of giving, another element of confidence is generosity. Giving to others helps us feel useful, gives us joy, and makes us feel like we have a purpose. How we give and who we give to is up to our personal preferences. Some like to donate to charity, others their religious organization, and still others like to give personally—to friends, family, even strangers. Have you ever noticed the glowing pleasure you feel when you give a gift to somebody? It's just plain good for us. Keep in mind, of course, that we would be nothing at all if we lived only for ourselves. We don't just want to improve our own lives, but also the lives of those around us. And it doesn't have to always be people, we can give to the earth as well. As a woodsman myself, there's nothing I like better than nurturing the land, helping it to be bountiful, help animals and plants to have an easier time. Not to get off topic, as this is no environmental book, but the next new housing development may seem to be an improvement to some people, but to the untamed denizens of that land it is a cataclysmic disaster that spells the end of the land that feeds them and made them in the first place.

A good part of the time, because of our busy lives, we have no time to rest and reflect in silence. When we are down or depressed, our mental vision has been clouded, making us unable to see things for how they are. No matter how troubled your life may be, there is ever so much to be grateful for. Instead of always lingering on the things that go wrong, why not list in our mind all the good things that happen each day.

Life itself is a wondrous miracle, with all its little details: the wind rustling in the treetops, the birds singing, a breath of fresh air, the smile of someone you love, even the way you move your fingers! What? Yes indeed, your body is an amazing thing, the unfathomable complexity of it, the dynamic movement we enjoy. Please try an experiment with me. Just look at the palm of your hand. Flex your fingers a couple times. Isn't it amazing to see how the tendons stretch at will by the unseen, unthought command of electrical signals in the brain?

Open your eyes each new day and see the world as if it were new, everything in it is completely unfamiliar. See the world as a child sees it, fascinated with the littlest, seemingly trivial things (in the eyes of an adult), exploring nature with fresh and twinkling eyes. Going out in the woods can help you see all this clearly. I do it all the time, the woods (or any wild place) soothes the soul. When in times of silence in the wilds, I'll ponder over such things. What was before a murky path will be laid open and bright before me. And if there's an unanswered question hanging yet in my mind, it will inevitably be answered soon as I step into the untamed land and out of mankind's chaotic creations. If you have no land on your property, perhaps find a peaceful park, or better yet, a graveyard. Believe me, traffic may constantly flow in and out of city parks, but it seldom is crowded in a graveyard, except for the dead—and it sure is quiet. Sorry to end on that note, but the sum of what you should remember from this chapter is this: we are what we make of ourselves. If we think small, we'll stay small, if we have grand ambitions, we will likely accomplish them. If we don't believe in ourselves, we will be weak and get nowhere, but if we do believe in ourselves: I can assure you, you will remain free and accomplish your purpose in happiness.

Chapter 2: Persuasive Techniques, First Impressions, and Body Language

What kind of first impression do you make? Do your eyes dart around, do you give a handshake like a wet dishrag, do you wear bedraggled clothes or a hoodie, slouch over and walk like somebody screwed your joints together a little bit loose? Hopefully not! Why? Because, by golly, that would make a terrible first impression. Your prospective employer, friend, or otherwise would likely take you for a hoodlum. Many people nowadays are never taught how to give a good first impression. But it's necessary to do so because it will shape their whole perception of you for a long time and can make or break your plans. As such, let's go over some important points to keep in mind.

Handshake. If you go up to somebody and give them a handshake like you've got no bones in your hand, they'll take you for an unreliable person. To give a good handshake, always lean on the side of too tight rather than too loose. Try and match or slightly exceed the grip of the other person. It should be firm, but don't treat their hand like a squeeze ball for stress. Remember, it's no contest. If you want to have a thumb war or arm wrestle, do it on your own time. Don't try and see who can squeeze the hardest; and if the person is elderly, please don't break their hand! Everything in moderation.

Posture. Don't slouch; you'll seem shifty and disrespectful. Stand up straight like a pine tree and walk with a broad, robust stride. You can by all means, keep your hand in your pocket, but don't put the hand all the way in, and definitely don't put both in. Remember, perception, perception, perception. It might sound silly, it might be unreasonable, and you might not like it, but it's just the way it is. Use it to your advantage.

Eye contact. If you look at the ground and dart your eyes around, you'll seem nervous, insincere, and untrustworthy. You may well be nervous, but you don't need to proclaim to everybody! Look them straight in the eye and don't look away, let them look away. In casual conversation, there's nothing wrong with looking around as you talk, but formal discussion demands strict eye contact. If they choose to look away, let them, just don't you do it. Steady eye contact denotes integrity, dignity, and reliability to people. You certainly want to reflect those virtues.

Dress. A rule I've heard is: in a job interview, dress one level above what you'd generally wear at the job. If you're being interviewed to be a farm worker, you don't need to wear a three-piece suit, in fact, to do so would invite too much attention and possibly ridicule. For example, if you're being interviewed for a carpentry job, nice jeans and a button-down shirt, perhaps even corduroy pants, would do fine. You likely will wear worn and faded work pants while working, but you want to put your best foot forward.

Speech. Colloquial language, if not vulgar, is probably fine. The main rule of thumb is to try and reciprocate the language of the person you talk to. If they are formal, you act formal; if they are laid back, you should be relaxed, too. Be all things to all people. Even if you are used to cursing, it may not offend you, but you can safely assume that it will bother others. Of course, there's nothing inherently wrong with particular verbal sounds. If I moved to Ethiopia and learned to speak Amharic and there was some word in that language that sounded exactly like an English curse word, I wouldn't refrain from saying it, it wouldn't bother me at all. Why? Vulgarity is all about the connotation, or feeling that the word conveys; in other words, the power we give the word. Many people sprinkle curse words into every other word they speak.

They curse when they're happy, they curse when they're sad, they curse when they're laughing, and they curse when they're mad. Curse words are just a crutch that people lean on for lack of meaningful vocabulary. The curse word may mean nothing to you, but it may be shocking to somebody else. Do be careful to bridle your tongue.

Persuasive techniques are a useful tool that helps convince people of your viewpoint. It is good in an argumentative debate, when pleading your case for forgiveness, and even making employers interested in hiring you. You have to stand out from the crowd; you have to be a needle in the haystack. If you don't distinguish yourself by your principled virtues and impressive competence, you rely merely on chance that you may be chosen for a job, friendship, courtship, etc. There are several persuasive techniques you can use and some to avoid; we'll go over them one by one.

Let's start with the three most general and commonly used ones. First is Pathos. Pathos is useful and has its proper place, but it is unfortunately relied upon too heavily these days. It is an appeal to emotion, sentiment, and feelings. Its goal is to stir up strong feelings in somebody's heart in order to steer their thinking in your desired direction. Here's a common example: have you ever seen those ASPCA animal rights commercials? If so, you'll recall the sad music, the unusually dirty and deformed dogs, and the pleading voice asking for your donation. Now it's certainly a worthy cause, but the argument is based on your feelings, not reason. It hopes you will be moved with pity and sadness for these poor animals and will conclude the best course of action is to donate to the ASPCA. Another example of this is pharmaceutical commercials. These, you will notice, show beautiful weather and play upbeat music, portraying healthy-looking people participating in jolly, enjoyable activities. The intention is to capture your attention and direct it to all the pleasant scenes they portray; and even more important, to distract your attention from the drug's ingredients and the remarkably fast-paced voice outlining all the disturbing side-effects. Sound familiar? Unfortunately, most big news outlets rely on emotional bluster to get the point across, and it works. If you are trying to influence dull-witted or tired people to your side, this is undoubtedly by far the best technique. Such a strategy will not appeal, though, to logical people too well, which brings us to the next point.

Logos. Logos is an appeal to logic or reason. It avoids emotionality and primarily focuses on cause-and-effect scenarios that attempt to argue that a certain course of action is the most prudent. An example of this is gold buying commercials. You might not remember such commercials, they were more common in the past. But the general idea is that the value of the dollar (fiat currency) is going down, inflation is going up, and an economic downturn seems just around the corner. As gold does not lose value, rather, has been gaining value, it is a wise investment to purchase for an uncertain future. This technique is reasonable and admirable, but the only problem with it is that many people simply don't like to think, they like to be spoon-fed thoughts from others, and such reasoning may go over their heads, in which case you might try and simplify the idea to get the point across. Methodically explain the reasoning step by step, asking questions along the way—this will definitely help them understand most of the time.

The third technique is Ethos. Ethos is an appeal to principle, ethics, and morality. Of course, right off the bat you can discern that such rhetoric would not work on unprincipled and immoral people, but thank goodness, most people do not completely fall into that category. Much political and almost all religious rhetoric involves Ethos, calling on people's morality to guide their path of decision-making.

Another related principle is the subject of honor. Honor is usually framed within an official or unofficial code of honor, which sets the standard for respectable behavior. The early colonial United States had a very strong culture of honor which dictated many activities, historical and even present-day. Some sections of the United States and the world in general still have this culture of honor, especially in traditional, religious, and rural communities. All men and women of honor are careful to avoid giving direct counsel to someone, usually speaking very generally in the third person—seldom addressing the recipient directly. Also, insulting someone even in a small way, is strongly avoided unless somebody wants to end up in a verbal or physical altercation.

In the old days, even a mild insult quite often became a duel that resulted in the death of one man or the other. Thankfully, few of us ever have to fear this outcome, but it is nevertheless a wise course of action to craft your words carefully if you want to appeal to people. Honor also incentivizes people to maintain a highly respected reputation in their community. In some cases, this can lead to insincere people becoming obsessed with appearances, hiding their true darker nature from others, but that is a clear misuse of honor. Truly honorable people stand up for what they believe in, fight for it tooth and nail to their last breath, and remain impeccably aligned with their principles no matter what difficulties it may bring them—regardless of convenience. Wherever you come from, whatever culture, whatever background: are not these certainly high-minded ideals we can all aspire to?

In addition, when we are trying to convince people of our view, we need to keep in mind some argumentative fallacies we do best to avoid. Now, do remember that if your argument does contain a fallacy, fallacy does not mean "inherently false." And it certainly wouldn't falsify your whole argument—it only means a weakness that could be criticized by opponents. With that in mind, let us proceed.

Bandwagon. The bandwagon fallacy is a psychological technique people use to make you feel left out. It implies: "Everybody is doing something, so you should do it too, don't get left behind!" Children use this habitually: "Hey Bo, how about we get you a smoke?" Says Bo, "Nah, Frank, I don't know about that. My ma got lung cancer smoking." Says Frank, "Oh come on, everybody's doing it!" Poor Bo. What significance is in the number of people doing a thing, and why it matters, I don't have the slightest idea. The true standard by which we should make decisions is logic and reason, even if we're the only ones doing it, if we believe it's the right thing to do, do it.

Next up is the Strawman or red herring. In the middle of a discussion, sometimes an individual with a disadvantage in the argument will toss out a red herring. A red herring or strawman fallacy is when someone inserts a random comment into a conversation in order to distract attention from the subject at hand. An example: John is the owner of a logging company, and he is interviewing a possible new employee. John says to his interviewee, "So Jim, do you got some experience in wood cutting?" Says Jim, "I love burning wood, my house has a nice wood stove, and it keeps us warm all winter." John responds, "Um, that's nice, Jim. Do you got any wood-cutting experience, though?" Jim's random interjection did not at all answer John's question. He only said it because he didn't want to answer the question.

Politicians especially can have the bad habit of refusing to answer questions and instead babbling on about nonsense that has nothing to do with what was being talked about. Another mistake politicians can make that you should never pick up is driveling. They are skilled at using many words to say practically nothing at all. If you have a complex idea to articulate, you may by all means, use fancy technical jargon, but never do it just to sound smart because a truly intelligent person will notice and take you for an idiot. If you are a fool, don't try and hide it, it only makes things worse. A fool is acceptable, a lying fool is not.

Another fallacy, the slippery slope. The slippery slope fallacy is when someone makes an unsupported assumption that if things continue as they are, they will inevitably lead to something unexpected. For example, "If loggers keep cutting down the Amazon Rainforest like this, it'll be gone in 20 years!" This was a statement many "experts" were making a few decades back. Clearly though, the Amazon is still intact, though as civilization continues making inroads into the forest, it has begun to be fragmented. The truth is that most slippery slope arguments actually have some validity, but you cannot just assume, you must have evidence for the result you believe will happen.

Circular Reasoning. This fallacy is another way people can sound smart as long as no one listens too carefully. It is when somebody attempts to explain their point but simply repeats the sentiment in different words. For instance, "I am a pretty good speaker because I express what I want to say very well." It might sound fine at first glance, but you notice the latter part of that sentence essentially means: "I am a good speaker." So in reality, what I am saying is this: "I am a good speaker because I am a good speaker." See how you think I was going to say something new there, but then I just repeated myself? It's like a circle, and thus the name—

circular reasoning. Clearly, repeating what you just said is not a strong or convincing argument.

Next, the No True Scotsman fallacy. Let's head right into the example with this one. Hannah says, "No man says the word 'fabulous.'" Mary responds, "Johnny says 'fabulous' all the time!" Hannah's retort: "Johnny must not be a real man then." Do you get the point? Good, then let's move on.

The Texas Sharpshooter fallacy is best described by the origin of the name. A Texan wanted to prove he was a real good shot with his squirrel rifle, so he fired a few bullets into a wall. Afterwards, he drew a target on the wall—with his bullet-holes right in the middle of the bullseye! Scientists and researchers can be tempted to cherry pick data to support their hypothesis despite the fact that the whole rest of the data disagrees with the hypothesis. A practical example of this: Scientist Sam says: "I believe more trees are dying than average because we've been getting more rain. I tested recently-killed trees and found that they had more moisture around their soil than living trees. That proves it." His colleague says, "Well Sam, there's lots of reasons that might be. Anyhow, we had a drought this year." Our Sam had his hypothesis, but failed to address all the data.

Now that we've gone over argumentative logic, let's dive into body language. Body language is a universal form of communication, though it does vary widely from species to species. Non-human animals use body language much more extensively than humans, though such animals still usually make use of vocal language. Think of birds singing, dolphins clicking, and so forth. Humans, on the other hand, are not as fluent in body language, often even oblivious to it.

An example of a man who defied that pattern was Monty Roberts; Monty Roberts grew up in a rodeo family and often participated in horse training, but from an early age, he seemed to disagree with the traditional horse training methods, seeing them as cruel and breaking the spirit of a horse. When he had the opportunity, he traveled from his home in the Salinas Valley of California to the High Desert of Nevada. There, he watched the movements of wild mustangs, but he noticed something that most people did not— their body language.

He was completely colorblind, seeing only black and white, and for that reason, he was more sensitive to movement. He eventually learned the consistent body language of all horses, wild or tame, which he calls Equus, and he uses it to his advantage in gently training horses. What may seem to be an impediment, that is, complete color blindness (seeing in black and white only), ended up being an advantage to Mr. Roberts, letting him see the world differently. Though he may have discovered this special method of horse training, which he calls "Join-Up," many other horsemen around the world use it as well. In fact, it became so popular in the equestrian world that the late Queen Elizabeth II of England invited him to show his method to her. In the same way, if we are careful to observe the body language and subtle movements of the people around us, we will better understand them and appeal to them. It can be simple enough by context and observation to discern the internal feelings of others; doing so will help us be more empathetic.

The most obvious and apparent form of body language is facial expression. In the Western World at least, politeness dictates we ought to look people in the eye, and therefore we notice facial expressions better than anything else. Despite this, focusing on only one detail can blind us to what else may be going on, so we're better off paying attention to a variety of signs.

Happiness and excitement can be discerned by observing the general energy with which they walk: that is, broad and quick strides. Also, lips will be upturned in a grin, the muscles on the cheek will be strained upwards and somewhat wrinkled, their eyes will be likely to be turned upwards as they walk, their eyes will squint and wrinkle at the corners, and the person's voice will likely be louder, faster, and higher pitched. Hopefully, this will be the expression you see most often!

Sadness is quite the opposite of happiness, both in subjective sensation and appearance. Their voice will be low, slow, and quiet; their face will droop with eyes slightly closed and looking downwards, cheeks relaxed, and lips turned down in a frown. Along with all that, movement will be slowed and dragging.

Anger is similar to sadness but much more intense. There will likely be a strong frown and furrowed eyebrows that extend the wrinkle into the forehead. Unlike the slow and suppressed movement of sadness, the movement will be fast, the voice loud and low, and the stare intense. Yelling, wild gestures, and violence can go hand in hand with unbridled wrath.

Focus is often indicated when a person locks their eyes on one thing, scrunching their eyebrows together and almost frowning. They will have a strong determination to get the job done and may become more impatient or irritable if anybody hinders their work. Focus can be manic, done in desperation, and associated with anger and stress. On the other hand, focus can be enjoyable and indicate the person has a purpose and enjoys participating in the activity they're engaged in. Another sign of focus can be observed while conversing with somebody, if they look upwards and move their eyes back and forth, this denotes they are trying to recall something (and may possibly be ignoring what you're saying to them). A lack of focus could take many forms. The person's eyes may drop, and their posture may look lethargic. Another common thing to see is when somebody has wide eyes looking out into space, which denotes a lack of enthusiasm and profound disinterest, shock, or dissatisfaction with whatever is going on. Stress is very similar to focus in appearance (albeit in a negative, manic form of focus) and may also involve nervous mannerisms like wringing the hands, twirling the hair, or running the hands through the hair on either side of the head and pressing into the temples.

Confidence is similar to happiness in most respects, and a truly happy person will usually be confident, so the two go hand in hand. They will make eye contact, speak forcefully and assertively, not doubtful of their abilities.

Fear is quite easy to notice because a person's natural inhibitions fly away in the face of terror. They may scream, cower, raise their cheeks without squinting the eyes (same as one would do when in pain), their lips could be clasped tightly shut, their posture is rigid, goosebumps may form, and gasping is quite likely.

The body language of dishonesty is often attempted to be hidden by the lier, but can be done sloppily, and thus a keen-eyed person can spot it. The person may lower their eyes, dart their eyes around, act shifty and fidgety, along with a very rigid posture. Another sign of lying is overdoing it, trying so hard to act truthfully that it becomes evident that the person is trying to hide something. Despite the fact that these may be common signs of dishonesty, there are plenty of other reasons why one may act this way. As such, it is always a good idea to give people the benefit of the doubt; if you can assume good or assume bad, then assume good. Try to see the best in people, and don't be suspicious or jealous. Don't let yourself be led along, but don't be overly cautious either. And when you associate yourself with people, try to take note of their honesty or lack thereof; you would never want to be stuck with an untrustworthy friend, or worse yet, an untrustworthy spouse. Do not choose your friends for superficial reasons because you may well regret it later.

Another type of body language, the type that is most often mentioned, is the cues that can occur between the opposite sex during courtship. A question that many young people ask during such a time is: "Does [so-and-so] like me?" Well, here are some pointers that could help answer that question.

A flirtatious pose is obvious, there is no mistaking it, and as such there is no reason for me to describe it—it varies greatly from person to person. Therefore what I will describe are the more subtle cues, those that can be mistaken. Sometimes, neither person may even realize they are exhibiting these signals. You should be aware of them so that you can avoid doing them if you don't want to, or that you can notice them in others as you interact. Most important of all to keep in mind is that these are not sure signs by any means. Many of these mannerisms are simply common in kindhearted people, but if you notice them in somebody that only exhibits them towards you—that would be the true sign that they have a deeper care for you.

If you mention to this person a little thing in passing, something you wouldn't expect them to remember, and they later repeat it to you or ask you a question about it, that shows the person is paying very close attention to what you say and do—indicating either that the person is very observant and possesses a good memory or that the person cares very much about you and made sure to take a mental note of what you said.

Attraction. Do they linger around you all the time and work with you if at all possible? Or they may even choose to avoid you in order not to bother you too much, in which case you may not notice. They may also take every opportunity, even when it is inconvenient for them, to talk with you, to check on how you're doing, and contact you through texting or calling you. This indicates that the person is frequently thinking about you and has a strong desire to be with you all the time.

Posture. The person will smile, stand straight up, with arms not crossed, hands either in the pockets, on the hips, or hanging at the sides. Their feet will face you directly, not turned at all to the side. They may brush against you frequently or touch your arm or shoulder. They will keep prolonged eye contact with you the whole time you are talking together, not turning away very often. Blushing is also a common indication of attraction. Blushing is caused by the release of various chemicals throughout the body that makes one feel excited, redden the skin, raise heartbeat and body temperature, and cause sweating thereby. Now, a habit of working together always indicates two people like each other, but it may not necessarily mean they love you in a special way.

Voice. Nervous stuttering, awkward speech, constantly asking questions, and a lot of laughing without anything funny happening can be a clue of attraction in some less confident people. The male will soften his voice, making it slightly more high-pitched, whereas the female will deepen her voice. This universal tendency is not done in an exaggerated way, just enough to equalize the two different voices so that they synchronize in pitch, speed, rhythm. It's like a beautiful song where the desire is to reach harmony by compromising together. This is also something empathic people will frequently do with everyone, which is something we will discuss later.

Mimicry. Somebody that wants to appeal to you will subconsciously mimic your behavior, your accent, your expressions, your mannerisms, your stance, and your facial expressions. A more silly and poor attempt at this is when somebody pretends to like everything you like. Of course, if the two of you really have that much in common, all the better. But pretenses are never a good idea to maintain. Pretenses are like a mask, as long as it is realistic and believable, it goes fine, but as soon as the mask is taken off, the truth is revealed.

As aforementioned, please remember that all these subtle cues are signs of friendship, attraction, and care. Caring people will naturally do most of these things to everyone they meet, and not at all in a romantic way. But whether that care is friendly or romantic is often very difficult to tell. The only surefire way to know for certain is if they tell you or you ask them point-blank.

Chapter 3: Empathy

First of all, let's see what's the difference between empathy and sympathy. Sympathy is essentially pitying a person and wishing them well. For example, "Aw, Jarmy got rheumatism, poor soul! I hope the herbalist can help him." Sympathy is simply taking action to show your concern for the plight of another—empathy goes much deeper. Empathy is truly feeling what they're feeling, walking in their shoes. It denotes a connection so deep as to allow an exchange of emotions between two people. Sympathy is to "feel bad for" someone, whereas empathy is to "feel with" someone. Do you see the distinction here?

Now empathy is certainly a noble virtue of the highest degree, something which all people ought to pursue, but it does have its drawbacks. Anything in too great or too little in quantity can be out of balance; as the saying goes, "Everything in moderation." If we have extreme empathy for every unfortunate person we meet and every unpleasant situation we hear of, we will certainly be miserable. In the past, most people only knew of the news that went on in their own little neck of the woods, and every once in a while, they'd hear of something going on in a big city nearby. Nowadays, we have the world at our fingertips, quite literally. We have access to all the news from the whole world; and in a world such as this, there seems to be far more bad news than good. Nobody can take the whole world on their shoulders! Let us each bear our own burdens, and also help with the burdens of those near us, but we are incapable of bearing the whole world's troubles all by ourselves. Some people are naturally empathetic, they intuitively see the pain of those around them, and it hurts them. By all means, let's do all in our power to help others, but we cannot be brought down by the various evils that plague the world. We do best to be strong, rocky islands that laugh at the most vicious tempest as it violently dashes into the island's rocks, and yet no flood can wash it away. Nonetheless, too much empathy is a rare problem; more often is too little empathy the issue.

Now, if we are already empathic, good, but if not, how do we cultivate empathy in ourselves? One of the foremost reasons we might fail to show empathy is that we have trouble understanding the feelings of others. This could make people feel that you are uncompassionate, unfeeling, and harsh. A simple way to remedy this would be to imagine yourself in their situation, their background, their strengths and weaknesses. When I have found myself being inconsiderate to others, I will put myself in their shoes, and immediately my mistake is made clear. Remember that everybody has a different way of thinking, which could influence how they experience life. If you are tough as nails, a friend that is traumatized by what seems to you a trivial thing, could put a wedge between you and your friend. Consider instead how they think. Do you give people coffee the way they like it or the way you like it? The very basis of all religion and morality is to "do to others only what you would want them to do to you." If the Golden Rule is universally followed, there is little room for error.

But empathy should go beyond a mere feeling—it should lead to action. When a loved one is hurting, we can comfort them. When a friend, acquaintance, or even a stranger needs something, we do everything in our power to give it to them. Sympathy is just consoling somebody: "I'm so sorry, Jim. You have my sincerest condolences. If there's anything you need, just tell me." It's all good and well to wish someone well, but you know our poor fictional Jim here doesn't want to be a bother, he likely won't ask his friend even if he does need something. We have to take the initiative and give them something they'd like. We don't need to be rich to give a gift; a gift can be our time, our love, a visit, a conversation, some help in the house or on the land. Anything really can be a gift, but the gifts we give depend on a few things, which we will discuss next.

Each of us has different ways we prefer to show love and receive love. If we don't understand how other people feel about love, we may seem cold and uncaring. Here are a few ways people show love; most people prefer one of the following or a combination of a few.

Touch. Many sensitive and emotional people show love by touch, the most obvious way. They like to hug, kiss, touch, touch, and touch. To other similar people, these expressions of care are perfectly fine, but to others, it can be quite annoying and embarrassing. Sometimes, more logical people will perceive "touchy-feely" love as shallow and sappy, but this is not necessarily always the case. Some people are truly sincere in their physical love. As long as the love goes deeper than touch, it is fine. But our love should be based on more than words and hugs, it should be proven by how we treat others. I knew a family very well once who were very outwardly loving, very "touchy-feely," but they were not sincerely so. The father in the family was very demanding, particular, and judgemental; the mother was very negative, dishonest, manipulative, and loved to complain and bemoan her lot in life. In this case, hugs and kisses didn't really mean true and genuine love.

Words. Others enjoy being told they are loved and given gifts. They live off of encouragement and attention; if they don't receive it, they'll believe you don't love them. They'll expect you to give them your complete attention and all the spare time you've got. If you seem distracted when you are spending time with loved ones, if you don't give direct and continuous eye contact, if you leave even for a moment to take care of some business or something for work, they will automatically interpret this as you wanting to get away from them. I knew a lady who said that her father always said he loved her till one night when she was seven years old or so. He never said it again, and she believed that she had disappointed him somehow. She never felt loved, but rather that she was a responsibility that her father took seriously. We wouldn't want our loved ones to feel that way about us. Even if actions mean more to us than words, we need to take into consideration that not all people feel that way. It may seem silly to us, but can't we humor them and just say: "I love you?" It can be very hard to start doing something we're not used to, and there may be various reasons why this may be too much for some people—for now, at least.

Some folks, usually country women, show love through food. They do a good bit of cooking and are really good at it. Their recipes are passed down for many generations and are well-revered by the family. In some more traditional, old-fashioned, backwoods homesteads, the man will go out hunting, fishing, tending the herd of wild hogs, and tending the cornfield. The woman will take care of the garden and orchards, draw water, and do the cooking. That's how they show love—a literal labor of love. This is still more or less the way things are done in many backcountry households in the US and around the world. Some people live more primitive than that, and others live more modern, but the point is: in a self-sufficient clan, work is love, for work is how everybody stays on the right side of the dirt, if you know what I mean (nobody wants to be six foot under—in a casket, I mean).

The last group we have here are those who expect action from someone who loves them. To people like this, words mean nothing, words can be an act. Gifts, attention, and quality time mean nothing because anybody can pay a little money and give a little time to get something they want out of somebody else. And then, such people believe, when people get tired of you, they'll cast you aside. What really means something to them is the little things. Do you compromise with them, do you help them, do you seem to genuinely enjoy their company? Essentially, do you care about them for who they are, even when you ask nothing from them? That is what they're looking for, all the outward forms of love just seem to shield reality. When you help people and care about them out of the goodness of your heart, when you have nothing to gain—that is what is trustworthy. Such people are usually critical thinkers, stoic, calculating, and based on reason and logic, and personal experience. My grandfather was one such man. He never talked about love, seldom hugged or touched, but he'd show it by the concern he had for others and the way he'd help people at his own expense. I greatly admire the man and aim to follow in his footsteps in that regard, yet at the same time, be capable of showing love in different ways if that's what other people want.

Love should never be an act, a mask that you take on and off at will. It must be genuine and earnest; otherwise, people will see right through it. And as I said before: give people their coffee the way they want it, not the way you want it. Give people love how they like it, not how you like it. Yes, it can be a challenge, it definitely is for me, but it's necessary in order to be a happy and well-loved person.

Our goal is never to force people to do what we want, to manipulate them, to control them. Certainly not. Our goal is to just be a caring person; this will naturally result in winning friends and influencing them for the better. And I can tell you from experience, it really works. I truly do not mean to brag about what I'm about to say; I'm going to tell you this story only as an example so as to help you see the results of common kindness. In school, I showed myself to be a patient, gentle, quiet, confident, helpful, and happy person. When somebody looked like they were having trouble with something, I helped them and was gentle and compassionate all the time. But I wasn't always that way though; I used to be an occasionally immature, inconsiderate, rude, disrespectful, hot-tempered fellow. But I noticed that the people I most enjoyed being around were always mild and meek, so it was only right I should be such a person as well. It is not really all that complicated, none of us were born mean. Our subconscious trauma and unpleasant experiences lead us to bad habits of dealing with people, which become ingrained over time. If you've been unkind or not quite the mildest of people, you might think it would be fake if you started to be nice now. You might think it's too late, but I guarantee you, if you start being kind now, it'll feel natural. The people around you might be surprised, but I'm sure they'll be pleased, too. If you start being kind hearted now, you'll help yourself, not just your loved ones, friends, and acquaintances. If you are impatient and short-fused, consider this: if you made a mistake little or big, wouldn't you want to be treated with mercy and swiftly forgiven? Well then, give others the same.

How can we uproot deeply rooted and thoroughly ingrained habits from our personality? And more than that, how do we go beyond just "acting" kind to really "being" kind? How do we make loving kindness our very identity, so that our very presence is pleasant and soothing to all those around us? Sounds like a big thing to accomplish, but really, unkindness is unnatural, not kindness, so all of us have it deep inside somewhere.

Baruch Spinoza, the philosopher of philosophers, a 1600s Dutchman of Portuguese Jewish origin, determined how to overcome our baser impulses. He believed that a passive or subconscious impulse/emotion (an urge which we know we have, but do not want it, nor know why we have it) can be turned into an active/conscious emotion (a feeling we choose and are aware of) if we come to understand the reasons behind the subconscious emotion. Basically, he said that we could gain control over our habits and actions if we know the reason why we have them—the root cause.

As a personal example: when I was a young boy, I was much taller than my fellows, and I liked it. I loved being tall, and at the rate I was growing, the doctors projected me to grow to about 6'6". I was just an early bloomer, though, and soon stopped short. I hoped I would get another growth spurt, though. Shortly thereafter, my younger brother shot up past me and was soon over 6 foot, and I ended up being a good 8 inches shorter.

Now I was looking up at my "little" brother, and everybody that knew us pointed it out constantly, every time we saw people they'd mention how my brother had outgrown me. Now, this really did bother me profoundly. But later, I began to understand that height doesn't decide your athletics, character, ability, or much else. I had been thinking of height as a competition, something that would give me an advantage. I realized that I had certain perceptions of what a "real man" should be. I couldn't imagine my future wife being taller than me, it mortified me at just the thought!

It was a real hangup for me, I was very wrapped up in height, but when I realized that my obsession with height was silly, didn't matter, and was unfounded, I stopped caring whether or not my brother was taller than me or whether women were taller than me. I even stopped caring when people that knew us pointed it out. I started to laugh about it.

So when this happened, I was walking in the woods in the crisp, cool, vibrant Fall time, and I was pondering over all these things. Surprisingly, the very moment I realized this, all my perturbations regarding my height instantly disappeared, and I actually began to appreciate my height. All the various benefits of being shorter dawned on me right then. I felt content immediately. A subconscious imbalance that had been limiting me, something I never realized was affecting me so much— disappeared in a blink of an eye just because I realized why I felt that way. That can happen to you, too. You'll never know how much the depths of your mind can affect your life, for better or worse, unless you take the time to do what I did. Get yourself out of whatever building you are currently in, get out in mother nature (forgive me if you already are outside), and reflect on your life. Being constantly distracted and entertained is a good way to interfere with your clarity of mind. Take a break from doing all the time, and start just being.

That brings us to the subject of mindfulness and meditation. Mindfulness sounds simple but can be difficult. It is living in the present moment, thinking of only one thing at a time, not letting your mind dart off to other things. When you're walking, think only of the movements of your body and your surroundings. When you are washing your hands, think only of that. When you are thinking or pondering, perhaps planning for the future (nobody expects you to never think ahead at all), then do nothing else and focus on thinking. Imagine your mind as going to war. When you think of many different things, you are sending parts of your military force off in different places, spreading them out, dividing them. An army is never as strong when it is divided. We want our minds to be like a focused, unbreakable, invincible force to be reckoned with, one that marches altogether. Unite the thoughts within your mind to accomplish enthusiastically whatever you may be doing. So you are reading now, then think only of reading and read with all your might. You may eat a meal hereafter, then don't let yourself eat for comfort, don't overeat, focus on that one activity, and you will feel when your body is content. If you are running, think of nothing else, run with all you might. That is mindfulness, and you really cannot be stressed out when you are completely mindful. Your mind will never grow weary, get frazzled or frayed, no, it will be at peace and in focus.

Meditation is done in many ways. Some people meditate on a sacred text such as the Bible or some other sacred book, others meditate on their breath, others meditate while looking at a light, some meditate on some sound or mantra, others meditate on visualizing some image or scenario, some meditate on their heartbeat, and it goes on and on and on. People tend to believe that their form of meditation is the only true form, but is that really true? All the forms of meditation I listed above have a commonality: a fastener. What is a fastener? If you were in a fishing boat and you wanted to stay in one spot for a long time, what would you do? You'd cast down the anchor, and that would fasten you to one place until you were ready to raise the anchor. If you were tanning an animal hide and you needed to hold the skin in place in order to scrape the fat off, you would tie it in place around a frame. If you're camping and you set up a tent, you'd drive tent pins into the ground. If you want to keep wood in place, you nail it together. In the same way, if you want to direct your mind toward one thing only, in complete focus, you need a fastener, you need to hold your mind in place, so it doesn't drift away. You need to tie it to one spot. In meditation, a fastener is something very simple that you focus on in order to empty your mind of everything unimportant. People have different goals with meditation, some more or less ambitious than others. Some people say they are emptying their minds of everything, but in meditation, that is almost never the case. The focus accomplished in meditation is always done by means of some fastener to hold you in place, something for you to figuratively hold onto; so meditation is essentially emptying your mind of everything but one thing, and that gives you the ability to focus like a laser beam on that one thing in order to have a more powerful mind capable of doing extraordinary things.

If you are unaccustomed to meditation, I'll recommend one way to you. The eyes actually have influence over your mind; when you are thinking intensely, your eyes will automatically dart around even with your eyes shut. You know Rapid-Eye-Movement Sleep (REM sleep)? That is a period of sleep in the latter part of the night in which dreams are most intense; it received its name because of the rapid darting around the eyes at this time. So here's the simple meditation method: while awake, hold your eyes at one particular point in the distance and un-focus them so that your vision looks blurry. Hold your eyes in that position for as long as you'd like, and you will be unable to think of anything. The focus of controlling your eyes and the fact that you will be purposefully taking advantage of their physiology will ensure that your mind is unable to dart around like it usually does. This is a good start.

But some might wonder: what do meditation and mindfulness have to do with empathy? A valid question, by all means because many people think of meditation as being merely a self-improvement strategy, but it is so much more than that. Meditation and mindfulness give you the ability to live in the present moment, which allows you to respond to your environment in a wiser way. Being mindful does not mean that your mind is "full," no, on the contrary, it means that your mind is altogether empty. Usually, while we drive, do house work, work in the fields, and any other activity we may think of as drudgery, we operate mindlessly, relying on muscle memory and previous experience to guide our actions as we let our minds drift off onto other subjects (as a side note: for anybody who wants an example of the subconscious mind at work, consider how you can drive for a while, get to your destination, and not even remember anything about the trip: your subconscious mind was at work).

Rather than letting our minds dart around while we vacantly do something without focusing on it, we'd do better to instead not to think at all. Consciously perform any task, and the little joys of life will return to you. If you walk past the same view every day and you no longer pay attention to it, focus instead on each step you take and the path ahead of you; you will see the beauty of it again. In the same way, we will automatically see how to treat others lovingly when we are living consciously in the moment. We will say to ourselves: "How could I have said that?" or, "How could I have thought that was acceptable before?" And we will have the opportunity to correct our course, to get back on the right path. Life is not the past, life is not the future, life is the present. Not the present year, not the present month, not the present day, but the very second or millisecond you are currently in. Yes, we must more or less consider the future to allow it to guide our present actions, and we do the same with the past, though we should never be limited by either. Live now like you'd want the future to be. Life is not a destination, it's a journey. If you can't enjoy the journey, then there's no purpose to life before you reach your goal, or even after you reach your goal! Purpose can only be found in the present. Don't wait for the perfect time to do something, that time may never come. Do not be shortsighted and brash, but neither be so methodical and lumbering and ponderous that you can never get anything done.

If you live in the present, you will still make use of logic and reason, but deep feelings and intuition will be your foremost guide. When you live in the present, you will notice things you never did before, see the world with fresh eyes, let go of your preconceptions, and feel for people, places, and creatures that never crossed your mind before. Living in the present is the key to all sorts of things because it gives you a clear mind, which enables you to see things as they really are, see your purpose, and act accordingly. I am still struggling to implement this myself, I am not perfect. It is a challenge in the modern world to get rid of distractions enough to focus on only one thing at a time. Some jobs and activities require multitasking, which is a great enemy of mindfulness. In order to see how to reduce distractions in our lives in a practical manner and see some ways of showing empathy, we will now discuss how to live a more simple, peaceful life.

We now have a good start for showing empathy for people, but what about the earth, our own native land and the creatures in it? Is not our compassion also due and appropriate for nature? In order to live compassionately towards nature, we may consider seeing how we could simplify our lives. We don't all need to be hunter-gatherers in the wilderness or even farmers, but we can minimize the harm we bring nature and maximize the benefit to it. Many environmentalists consider humans as a parasite upon the earth; this view I cannot agree with. Humans actually have the potential to be an important contributor to the balance of nature. Anthropologists that study Native American tribes have made some intriguing discoveries. Many tribes used practices intended to enrich the fertility of their land, limit their consumption of resources, and engender a respect in their people for the land, so that it was viewed as sacred. Because of these contributions, many Anthropologists consider pre-Columbian Native Americans to have been vital for the health of their ecosystem. After the indigenous population of the Americas was severely decimated by disease and war briefly following the early European settlement, this integral feature disappeared. As a result, various species went extinct. The point of my telling this informative anecdote is to prove that mankind need not be a sore on the face of the earth. We are a unique and amazing creature that has a very important place in nature. We can emulate that legacy. If you prefer not to simplify to the extreme, more moderate things might help.

Even influential elites, like Steve Jobs, chose a way of life called minimalism. Minimalism has occasionally been made fun of, but the core ideas are quite noble. The point is to remove distractions and excesses from life in order to simplify one's schedule, reduce financial stress, and open up more time to focus on what is more important to you.

Here's a suggestion: when you've gotten tired of reading my words, take a look around your house. Is there any junk laying around? Anything you could sell to get rid of? Anything you could do without? Anything you could consolidate to make life simpler? Riches and lots of things are only appealing in theory, in reality they only mean more to worry about and more to lose. Happiness cannot be bought, happiness comes from within, having and fulfilling your purpose in life. In Japan and China, many people sleep on a mat on the floor, people without water heaters take cold showers, some only use one big pot in the kitchen that all members of the family share, one fork, one spoon, and one knife. Turn off the climate control and open the windows (too chilly? Put on a jacket!), wear the same two or three pairs of clothes all the time (like Albert Einstein did), etc. We're all a work in progress, the more we learn, the more we can get rid of. You can apply this to whatever extent you like; I understand that this would be considered extreme by many people in the Western world. The point is not just to have little stuff; the point is to have more time, thought, and energy for the worthwhile things in life.

Chapter 4: How to be Pleasant to be Around

I have always been a very opinionated person, but in the past, I took this to the extreme. When I was younger, I used to have very strong sentiments about everything, and I would always insist on my way, I would never compromise with people. Just like everything else, compromise can be a delicate balance; it is easy to go too far in one direction or the other. Some people go along with whatever others tell them, not thinking for themselves, or even if they do think for themselves, they are willing to sacrifice their beliefs to appease others. It is true, we need to have principles, and we need to stand by them. If we believed something but never defended it, we'd be pushovers, cowards, and hypocrites. Those who insist on their way no matter what are often extremely unpleasant to be around; they just are not kind people. That refusal to compromise used to be how I was, but later on, I realized that acting like that repelled people away from me and made me unhappy. So I started being more yielding, I started going along with what people said. More people started liking me at that point, but I soon found myself occasionally giving up my principles in order to make others happy. I had to learn to find a happy balance with this.

The rule of thumb I came to understand is: to compromise with others as much as you can without sacrificing your morals. When we compromise with family, friends, coworkers, and others, it will likely not be what we prefer, it will not be ideal in our opinion, but it will make both parties a little happier. Be willing to make self-sacrifices to help others, but never make a compromise that would hurt yourself. For example, I had a strong distaste for toxic chemicals, but some in my family did not share this sentiment. They often would use them to clean things. Instead of attempting to force them to never use chemicals, instead, I let them do what they want and I would clean and wash what was mine how I preferred to do it. Occasionally, I would attempt to reason with them on the matter; sometimes it worked, and sometimes it didn't.

Sometimes, a family member would ask me to use some kind of chemical cleaner to do a "deep clean," and as long as it would cause minimal harm to me and the environment (when used properly), I tried to meet them halfway.

If the other person will not meet you halfway, they want it exactly their way; you have the decision to make—will you stick by your stance or give in? The right decision depends very much on you, the other person, and the situation you are in. One thing to remember, though, is something many people would never think of. Slavery is not just owning another person or being owned by a master, it can also be when you are ruled by an authority. You may even be ruled by yourself. For my part, I don't want to be a slave to anyone or anything. I refuse to be ruled by addiction, fear, pleasures, or anything else. As long as in the course of your compromising you constantly maintain your sovereignty over your own choices, you are doing well. If people see that you are doing your best to please them and yet at the same time you are a principled, moral, virtuous person of integrity, they will trust you, respect you, and admire your indomitable spirit. You will indeed be a pleasant person to be around, a real joy.

The truth is, that if you do not like your life or your personality, you have nobody to blame. We often will experience some trauma when we're young, and this will imprint in our minds. We will keenly remember this moment, it will shape our beliefs about ourselves, and the pain of it still stings. This trauma will often change us and change our life course. If we have problems in life, we're depressed, we lack self-confidence, we have hatred, fear, addictions, etc.—we tend to blame it on something that happened to us or somebody. "I am how I am because of so-and-so or this-and-that." We are better than that. We don't need to live in the past, we need to let go of it. You are what you choose to be right now, nobody can make you what you are. If you're depressed, you don't need to tell yourself that you're happy—that would be a lie! Just tell yourself the truth: you have great potential, you have a purpose in life, you have the potential to be happy, to accomplish your purpose, to live your dream—but only you can make it happen. Others can help you along the way, your faith and spirituality can also help you, but ultimately you have to make the choices.

If we are not natural leaders, that is fine, we don't need to be the boss of other people, but we do need to lead ourselves. We need to train ourselves as you would train a dog. Our bodies have a mind of their own, the body loves to stay in its comfort zone, stay within the bounds of the familiar. Even if the familiar is depression and sorrow, the body fears changing that! But we have the power to change that, the choice is ours. Your body tells you: "I know this sugary cake will make you feel terrible, but it is pleasurable, it is comfort food, so do it—do it for me!" It asks of us things that are seldom for our benefit. The body can get into good habits, good comfort zones, but the body is like a dog, it needs training. Sometimes, when one of my dogs was younger, I would give her some food, I would move my hand towards the bowl, and she would growl at me. She was afraid I would take her treasure. So me and my family started training her. We would give her the food, take it away from her, make her sit and stay, then give it back. She had to learn to trust us: "Yes, Dog, I'll give you your food, I'll give you your toy, but you need to calm down, trust me, and sit and stay for a while." Our bodies are the same way, we need to train them and love them. Believe me, the body really is an intelligence of its own, but it can be dull witted, so it needs to learn to listen to us.

Another important aspect of being a pleasant person is your charisma. Speaking softly, slowly, and gently is vital for people to feel comfortable around you. We want to be approachable people, so we would be wise to be calm, patient, merciful, and choose our words wisely. A smile and eye contact are some other obvious habits to maintain as you deal with others. You may be a quiet, friendly person, but if you don't talk to people, don't smile, avoid eye contact, and so forth, you may seem standoffish and aloof.

While I was in High School and in a certain class, I was once assigned to mentor a new student. He was told by our teacher to ask me if he needed help, to have me show him the safety guidelines before using each tool, and in general, to let me guide his work. I didn't make an effort to go to him and help him; instead, I waited for him to come to me for help.

Ultimately, he didn't actually come to me at all and as a result, had a difficult time on a project and broke quite a few safety rules. The day after, I apologized for not going over to help him out, I was busy with my own project, and from then on, I made sure to show him the ropes. He had pride and said he had been fine without help, but clearly thereafter, he appreciated some assistance. I was very kind, patient, and helpful with the boy, but I wasn't approachable because I didn't make the first move to get to know him or befriend him.

In the same way, you may miss friendships, courtships, and possibly even a potential spouse if you do not seem approachable to those around you. You should radiate an aura of kindness, truth, and integrity. It should be apparent to whoever you may be around. You may seem different, in fact, you will be different because most people are not like that, but they will admire you and be most likely to go to you and trust you in times of trouble. Of course, that is easier said than done!

In order to ooze kindness from your very being, you cannot just act kind; you must be kind in every aspect of life. When you drive in traffic, do you get annoyed and honk somebody, even if they may "deserve" it? When you watch the news, and you see politicians' trickery, hypocrisy, and treachery, do you hate them? Do you judge those who feel differently than you, and believe different things than you? Even if you don't show it, do your friends or family annoy you, do you bottle up that distaste? Are you bitter about the trauma and hardships that have occurred in your life, even if they are severe? These are serious questions worth careful reflection on all our parts because our answers to them reveal something important. Are we actors of kindness or are we kind, even to ourselves?

As discussed in the first chapter, if you lack self-confidence and are unkind to yourself, that will be reflected in your dealings with others. Do not suppose that you can hide internal bitterness; and would you really want to? Lying is hard, it takes constant maintenance, caution, and fabrication to keep up. If we are not as we appear, why not either show our true self or change our true self? Fakery is no option. To become a new person, we have to unmake the old. That takes a profound change in our attitude and mentality that takes work. People are seldom ever handed a better personality on a silver platter, it usually takes work. Yes, some people have spontaneous, life-changing, experiences from some epiphany or revelation that fundamentally and immediately change their whole mind. Most of us have not been so lucky. We don't have to have a miracle to change.

We will all continue to be a work in progress so long as we live, so we might as well start now. Many people have to experience tragedy and sickness to realize there's more to life. If we start improving ourselves and searching for the truth now, we will save a lot of time and prevent many problems.

When we feel a certain way about somebody, be willing to share it. If you are thankful for what somebody did, tell them. Politeness also goes a long way (Yes sir, no sir, yes ma'am, no ma'am, please, thank you, good to meet you, how are you doing, have a good day, hold the door for others, wave, etc.). Apologize when you do wrong; you will be respected for it, and people will draw closer to you. And make your apology genuine; nobody likes "I'm sorry you feel that way." If you say that, you're really just putting the blame on them, and it will do no good whatsoever.

Listen more than you talk, unless the other person hardly says a word, in which case it might be a good idea to "break the ice." Laughing makes everyone around feel better, and the same with complimenting others when appropriate. They don't have to paint the Mona Lisa or build the Taj Mahal to be worthy of a compliment. If there is no conversation, why not start one? One thing to remember is that asking personal questions makes people feel uncomfortable and may even annoy them, so avoid that. Include outcasts and welcome less popular people and you will earn a friend easily. Hold back from giving too much criticism unless the person knows you well and you sincerely believe it will help them. Perform random acts of kindness, even to strangers; if you have a general attitude of kindness in your life, you will naturally see opportunities to help others.

In the same High School I previously mentioned, the same student under my mentorship was feeling poorly for a couple days in succession. The class was doing a study of the textbook, and there weren't enough copies for everybody, and this fellow didn't have one. I saw that he would have trouble paying attention without a book and that would only make it worse when we had to take the test afterwards, so I gave him my book and said I'd be fine just listening. The teacher complimented me on that, and everybody seemed to have a high respect for me thereafter. Also, he and I became friends after that.

Another thing to try is "when in Rome, do as the Romans do." This is an old-timey adage that still holds true just as much as when first it was first said. It indicates that we do best to appeal to people as much as possible, to follow their lead. You wouldn't want to be obstinate and refuse to adapt to your surroundings. At the same time, you wouldn't want to constantly compromise your principles in order to please others. Just like everything else, it's a delicate balance, and it's easy to go too far in either direction. When you sense a certain "vibe" or way of thinking on the part of someone you're around, try not to contradict them.

For example, I am extremely critical of technology, I like to live a simple, natural life with minimal distractions. I will make use of technology if there is some practical benefit to it, but I will not squander my time with it. I have observed that we live in an extremely unadventurous society; adventure is mostly found in fictional novels and television shows at this point. Why might that be? In the past, adventurers and explorers abounded. One reason is that people attend mandatory schooling, which teaches them to think inside the box, not outside the box, and they are encouraged to pursue a conventional and respectable career that will make them "successful," in other words, make lots of money. People now measure success not by happiness or helping others, but by their paychecks. But the thirst for adventure and wonder still burns within their hearts; how do they satisfy this urge? They watch television shows of other imaginary people living adventures. They live through the eyes of others, they use television and books as a crutch, as a way of experiencing adventure without having to leave their comfort zones and put forth the effort of living adventure for themselves. They content themselves with the imaginary, to the fictional. A few hundred years ago, fiction was unheard of for the most part, it was considered lying to write fiction. Now fiction abounds, and adventurous people diminish. Now, do not suppose I am advising you against all forms of media. The news is just plain mind-numbing and depressing at this point; each of us have enough of our own problems, we have no need to take the whole world's problems on our shoulders by having to hear about them. Pure entertainment is just a diversion, a waste of time. On the other hand, a book, television show, or something else that inspires us to live our own lives more fully—that is definitely worth our time! The internet, though it has many drawbacks and disadvantages, allows us to have almost the entire mass of accumulated human knowledge at our fingertips. With great power comes great responsibility; let's use it wisely and not frivolously.

Anyway, back to my original subject: an example of appealing to people. I have been wary of technology ever since childhood, but my friends at the time hardly shared that sentiment. They, as are many young people nowadays, were utterly addicted to technology. When I dealt with them, I had to be careful to express what I would and would not do without insulting their sensibilities. I admit it was often like walking on eggshells or thin ice. Eventually, I slowly parted ways with these friends because we had hardly anything in common. That made life easier for me, in my opinion. But having no friends can be hard, too! I later gained many friendships, though they were all much older than me, that was just fine. Old folks need help and have a lot of wisdom to share, I can assure you.

Tiptoeing around sensitive issues with people can be quite tiresome! If it's worth it to you, keep up that fellowship. But if your chosen company is more trouble than it's worth, you might want to consider going separate ways. If you have to be around certain people, workmates, for example, do your best to "kill them with kindness," and they might just stop bothering you.

Speaking of that subject, I have something else to share with you. In school, I was around people that cussed like sailors, no, worse than sailors. They used curses so frequently that it lost all meaning to them, it became something they used in order to supplement their limited vocabulary. I never felt the need to do so, myself. These kids also had no morals whatsoever, and not surprisingly, they were often depressed because they had no purpose in life. When the school year started, and I was in class with lots of new people, they would at first treat me poorly. I was no weakling, and I was quite capable of defending myself verbally or physically, but I was patient with them and refrained from retaliating. Pretty soon, they began to soften and reciprocate the same kind, quiet way with which I treated them. I could see the difference in how they treated their peers and how they treated me, they learned to calm down and mirror my personality. They were unaccustomed to being treated with compassion and concern, and this confused them. Each one of them was born a kind person, but they imitated others and learned to act harshly. At first, when I had just started school, I made the same mistake, but later, it occurred to me that I wasn't a sponge, I didn't have to soak up whatever was near me; from then on, I never saw fit to copy the behavior of others. I have often seemed strange because I don't conform, but I'm also admired when people begin to understand why I choose to live the way I do. As a freethinker, the insights I've gained have led me to do many odd things, but I don't care what's normal; if it helps me and my family live healthier and happier lives, I don't think I'll look back once I'm old and say: "Boy, do I wish I'd done what everybody else did." I aim to have no regrets, so I refuse to be tempted to give up my dreams. If you have dreams, a vision, especially one that is for the betterment of mankind, pursue it ferociously because it is not very likely to plop right in your lap without some effort.

We have lots of followers in our world and not enough leaders. Even many of our "leaders" are actually followers. Learn to be your own person, work well with others, and yet at the same time, be willing to take the initiative to be the first to do something, even if there's nobody else leading the way to show you how— learn as you go. If we have more inspiring, charismatic, incorruptible leaders in this world, we would have a much pleasanter world.

As I mentioned before, we often know who we really are, until we go to school. Let's take a lesson from the illustrious Mr. Mark Twain when he said, "I never let my schooling interfere with my education, " and, "We have not the reverent feeling for the rainbow that a savage has because we know how it is made. We have lost as much as we gained by prying into that matter," and finally, "Education consists mainly of what we have unlearned." Indeed, schooling is a different matter than education; education is made of personal interests that we research and therein find revelations. I have realized many wonderful things by simply pacing back and forth in the woods, pondering over a seemingly mundane subject. Also, as children, not to be rude, but we are basically savages. At that early age, we instinctively understand many things about what's really important, but we are soon taught right out of that wisdom. Decades later, we might realize that what we instinctively did as children were exactly what was good for us—now we have to try and repair the damage done by a lifetime of ignorance induced by schooling and baseless traditions. More important than learning and coming to know something is this instead: unlearning what we've been taught and realizing we know nothing at all! The more I learn, the more I realize I don't know. Anybody you see who thinks they are wise: do not trust them, that's actually the best sign that they are ignorant. If they really knew something, they would be open to the possibility that they may be wrong. A genius is not somebody that understands a lot, it is someone wise enough to understand that we all are quite stupid. One more quote from Mark Twain: "Thousands of geniuses live and die undiscovered—either by themselves or by others." We all have a lot of potential, we just have to figure out how to realize our full potential.

When you have that sense of purpose, that balance, that confidence, you will naturally be admired by most who meet you. Just remember to never hold yourself above others with a sense of superiority. If you act like that, just as soon as they begin to admire you, they'll flee from you. Quite frankly, keeping a balanced attitude is plain hard. We're like pendulums in an old grandfather clock that swing back and forth from one extreme to the other, never staying in the middle. Being distracted, busy, stressed, and multitasking can make it easy to fail to realize if we are off track. What I've found always helps me to step back and take an honest look at my life as an unbiased observer is just going into an isolated spot, pacing back and forth, talking to myself, and meditating. Focusing only on one thing at a time, the thing you're currently doing (in other words: living in the present moment). Disconnecting from the constant busyness is a necessity. If you make good habits like that, you'll make yourself and others happy.

Chapter 5: Understanding Psychology

Making friends and influencing people (hopefully in a positive way) are generally thought to be mostly physical activities. What we say to people, how we act, do we try and make the first move in friendship, are we approachable, etc. But there are also some mental aspects to human relationships that, if neglected, could cause us trouble.

As the saying goes, "no man is an island." Everybody needs some form of interpersonal connection, some support. Even a hermit off in the wilderness has a connection to the animals, plants, and land that he dwells in. Have you ever seen the film Cast Away with the actor Tom Hanks? In it, the protagonist, Chuck Noland, experiences a plane crash in the Pacific and is stranded on a remote island. He faces many challenges attempting to survive and keep his spirits up, but he lacks a friend. In order to create a friend for himself, he takes a volleyball he found in a package from the crash, then paints a face on it from his own blood, and names it "Wilson," which is the company name written on the ball. He views the ball like a companion and talks to it extensively; of course, essentially he's really just talking to himself, but our human, innate need for companions led him to pretend. This helped him maintain his sanity and keep up morale in such a seemingly bleak situation. Hopefully, none of us will have to face such a hardship as that, though, it honestly might be nice to be stranded on an island as long as you had something to keep you company—whether that be an animal, plant, or human. In any case, no matter how introverted we may be (I am definitely one such person), just stay isolated from people for a while, and you'll realize that you have a psychological need for companionship of some kind.

Friendship can have a strong effect on your health, for better or worse. Peer pressure is an ever-present stimulus that leads us to feel the need to conform to the behavior of those around us. A good and kind group of friends will inevitably encourage you to be happy, to be positive, to take care of yourself physically, and to have something to look forward to. On the other hand, the wrong crowd can be toxic for us, mentally and physically. We all rub off on each other, whether we like it or not, so choose your friends wisely.

Friends will offer us support when we face troubles and can help us get through our adversities. When at work, whatever your job may be, companions can make the time go faster, make us more content, and help us work faster. When I worked on a local man's farm, the same grouchy, but kind fellow I mentioned before: working alone every day would have been absolutely intolerable. He was exhausting to be around, and not just physically; he wore me down mentally to a nub. Now don't get me wrong, I liked the work for the most part, but on days where I worked there alone... Goodness, the time dragged on endlessly. I checked my watch and always found that little time had passed. Sometimes I would weed fields on my hands and knees in the Sun all day long, and not sparse weeds here and there, but whole jungles of vegetation taller than me! I love plants, but goodness, if pulling weeds is murder, then I committed genocide on a mass scale. My joints in my fingers, knees, back, neck, and feet would ache from the long maintenance of that awkward position, I would switch back and forth between squatting until neither were comfortable anymore—I just had to get used to being constantly uncomfortable, which was good for me. When I had company to talk to, to work alongside, to get some help from: the time sure flew then. I worked quicker, had more laughs, and enjoyed the day far more. If I didn't quite understand what I was supposed to do, my workmates would help me, and I would do the same for them. The workload was less overpowering if there were multiple people helping; many hands make the load light. As a literal example of that, we once were lifting a huge, solid oak banquet table, but quite a few hands lifted it up, and we each felt like we were lifting just a cardboard box! Ultimately, I view that early experience as a good one, and I'm no weakling, but I honestly couldn't have done it by myself. I suppose I could've done it alone, but I likely would've just quit after a while instead.

You know the expression: "It takes a village to raise a child." We in our Western culture are very independent, relatively speaking. Most families are made up of parents and their children. They have no community, no tribe. They often have never met their neighbors. Yes, we may have our religious community, our work community, our extended family, and our casual friends, but our lives are very compartmentalized, very separate. In the old days, the people you worshiped were the same that lived side by side with you, worked with you, danced with you, sang with you, and loved you. Even their future spouses would be found in their tribe or village, everything and everyone they needed was within a close distance to them. This was a necessity in a world without cars and grocery stores, people needed each other.

Now, you can make money doing a job in an office, that money is sent in imaginary numbers to your bank account, you buy your needs and wants in a store or through the Internet, and you probably produce very little of your own food and do not really need your neighbors. You may be used to that lifestyle, but consider the possible advantages of a supportive community. We would be self-sufficient, we would pollute our lands far less, we would have less stress, etc., etc., etc.. Just think about that for a second, how would your life and the lives of your beloved family members benefit from a real community, a tribe? It may take a whole village to raise a child in the best way possible, but that's impossible if you have no village in the first place. Try to build a community, your own tribe, you don't have to make big changes if you don't want to, but just start being more friendly with your neighbors and see what happens.

If you want to find friends, but don't know how I'll give a few suggestions. Many people use social media, and they may have many online "friends." But they likely never spoke to many of these people, and certainly never met them face-to-face. Social media gives people the feeling of being "connected" while never actually having any personal connections. If you content yourself with friends you talk to with buttons, you may lose many of the benefits of real friends. Social media, I'm sure, can be useful for finding like-minded people, especially if your interests are obscure or unusual, but please, try to use social media only as a way of finding people to meet—don't just be penpals. Some other ways of finding friends may be to go to some local religious meeting, volunteer at some helpful community project, join a club, offer to help your neighbors with yard work (especially if they're elderly or unwell), or make friends with the people you work with.

It's no easy task to just go and start up a conversation with a stranger, so it might be easier to focus on being friendly with the folks you're around every day. But if you do want to strike up a conversation with a stranger, here's some basic pointers: smile, look them in the eye, compliment them on something to put them at ease, maybe ask them a question (if you don't think it will make them uncomfortable—don't put people on the spot), have a sense of humor, and if appropriate, perhaps ask them if you both could exchange contact information. In a small, country town, this process will be much easier because people are usually at ease there anyway.

If you already have friends and would like to keep the friendship thriving, here's a few things to keep in mind. Spend time with them. Don't suppose you can plant the seed of friendship, walk away, come back after a long time, and expect that plant of friendship to have grown. Friendships are what we make them, as such, we need to invest time, care, and effort. If we expect them to treat us with care, we have to treat them with care. Trust is also a necessity, but building trust can be hard. People generally begin to trust each other when they go through hard times together, they support each other all the way, and no temptation causes them to betray each other; their loyalties are tested, and they prove true every time, through thick and thin, bitter and sweet. But if we only have casual friendships and we do not rely on each other for anything whatsoever, how can we have such close friendships? Well, honestly, nothing can approximate going through hard times together. There is a special attachment there that cannot be imitated.

Did you ever see the Lord of the Rings trilogy of films based on J. R. R. Tolkien's masterfully-made books? If so, you'll recall that throughout the story, the protagonist, Frodo, and his friend, Sam, became progressively closer as they leaned on each other during their long, perilous, and fearful journey. At one point, Frodo attempted to go off on his own to finish the worst part of the trek; he didn't want anybody else to have to bear his burden with him. Despite this, his dear friend Sam chased after him and insisted upon going with him—they'd come this far together, and they would finish together: there was no other way. Later, near the end, climbing the blistering hot slopes of an evil mountain and hiding from the eye of their great enemy, you can perceive the way that the sheer intensity of facing all these hardships had drawn them together. The best of friends can only be produced by intimately living side-by-side, in good times and bad times (which is why, when such a relationship fails, it is far more devastating than a more superficial one).

Nonetheless, being there for your friend, even in the little things, for a long time—will lead you to a close friendship. And not to be negative, but in the worsening, dark, bleak, and divided world around us, we may just end up going through some hard times. Economic concerns, wars overseas, unusual illnesses—we've already experienced those. But let's be real, most of us have faced no real cataclysm, no severe calamity, no mass catastrophe. We have our individual and family problems, but nothing like what could happen. What is probably about to happen... So let's be thankful for this, and though I'd never wish a worldwide catastrophe on anybody, if such does come to pass, I have no doubt that we will band together and unite to face whatever comes.

The increasing divisiveness and contention between those of differing opinions in our society is becoming more polarized all the time—and that may affect our friendships. It may be hard to relate to someone of a drastically different mentality. Of course, we should be civil and kind to anybody we meet, but we may choose not to pursue a friendship with those who think too differently from ourselves. Such relationships can last a little while, but the whole time, each of you will be walking on eggshells to avoid insulting the other person or sharing your personal opinions that would bother your friend. Eventually, such relationships universally tend to lead to estrangement and separation. Now, don't suppose that just because someone has differing views than you, that this person must be evil—that would be unreasonable and imbalanced on your part to make that brash assumption. Consider how their family, background, and upbringing may have led to their views. You may not agree, but at least you should learn to understand where they're coming from.

In particular, politics, religion, and now personal medical preferences (you probably know what I mean, though I don't want to get into detail) are big controversies; they can be very divisive topics. It may be wise to avoid discussing them unless you know you are with a like-minded person or group.

Politics used to be a dry subject regarding economics and suchlike, the kind of thing that old men in black suits would discuss in a dimly-lit board room while smoking their pipes. The point is that it was not an exciting topic that the average person would be interested in, and certainly young people used to care little or nothing for politics. In the past, most people agreed on what their political, common goal was, but they just disagreed on how to accomplish that goal. Nowadays, things have taken a different turn: politics are now based on moral, religious, and scientific issues, and nobody even has a common goal. I know you've probably heard something like this before, but what do people usually say next? Usually they say something along the lines of: "I wish people could just agree on things and believe in common sense. You know, I pretty much wish they'd agree with me." I will not say that to you because that would defeat the whole point of condemning our polarized world. If I said that the solution to our political problems was everybody agreeing with my views, wouldn't that just make the problem worse?

The problem is not just the polarization of politics, but also the fact that people can't seem to understand that they don't have to hate "the other side" or "the bad guys." We are not in a sports competition, we're not in a literal military war (yet), though we certainly are in an intellectual war. Let me warn you, from a thorough study of history, you will undoubtedly find that our society is following the telltale steps towards collapse, anarchy, and war. "A house divided cannot stand," and I guarantee you that for numerous societal, cultural, religious, and environmental reasons, our society is destined towards calamity if something does not suddenly change. I'm sorry to say that, but we are not immune to history, the modern world follows the same age-old patterns, but I want you to know that this is our choice: we can change it. That change would start with our refusal to demonize those who feel differently than us, our refusal to treat them as enemies, and our willingness to move outside the bounds of our "team" to do what we believe to be right and to make friends. Our goal is to work towards the common good, not to stick with our "team" no matter what, and choose to hate those who disagree with us. We can make friends with those who disagree with us. The question is: are you willing to?

Tribalism is an unusual topic in sociology and psychology. On one hand, we observe that people thrive better when they have the support and fellow feeling of a tribe or clan, but on the other hand, unfortunately, tribalism, in certain types of societies, can create competition and strife between different groups which leads to violence, hatred, warfare, and petty feuds. We can see that in our society. Even with something so trivial, in the grand scheme of things, as team sports can pit people against each other to the point of violence. I once heard of a fan of one American football team who heard a nearby fan of a different team cheering, which angered the former individual to an extreme degree. He then proceeded to approach that other fan and brutally beat him to a pulp, almost killing him. Of course, he was prosecuted and jailed. Honestly, let's think about that for a second. You understand that

American football teams are franchises that have team members from all over the country, most are not even from the area that the team claims to represent. In addition, teams will occasionally move to a far away location if it appears to be more profitable, proving that the team is just a business and not in any way loyal to any particular place. And yet people can become so obsessed with watching these games and rooting for their team that it tears their friendships apart.

Where I lived as a child, I would frequently see signs on many people's doors that said: "A house divided," and it would show a picture underneath split in half, with each side showing the emblem of one of the two popular football teams in that area. I actually would see kids in school occasionally coming to blows over this issue. I will not mince words over this: such an attitude is insane, idiotic, and inexcusable. In all honesty, fans of team sports tend to be more hateful towards the other side than the actual sports players are! The reason for that is that football is just a job to them, maybe even a passion, but as they personally know many players from other teams, they do not feel the need to treat them with contempt (though of course there are exceptions to this when a brawl occurs). The fans are not even playing the game, they're just watching others play it, so the great mental investment that fans put into their team is unreasonable, illogical, and unfounded in reality. I do not mean to insult those who feel this way, but our world has enough real hatred and controversy that it seems silly to create imaginary controversy over team loyalty in sports. But psychologically speaking, we all have a desire to have a community of like-minded people, a tribe, a group to support us and work together for the common good.

As I mentioned before, because of our modern lifestyle, our communities are fragmented; our church or religious community is seldom made up of the same people as our work community, our work mates are seldom ever our next-door neighbors, and our next-door neighbors are seldom our best friends or family. This separated and fragmented society is symptomatic of the mental trauma, confusion, and psychological imbalance that modern life has afflicted us with. But we do not have to be "victims," we can choose whether we follow the crowd in groupthink or whether we follow our principles like free people.

Remember though, we can try to do it alone, and we may not do so shabby, but we cannot reach our full potential without the support of others. Perhaps you've heard of the historical Mountain Men who left "civilized" society in the 1800s in order to roam free over the Rocky Mountains and other wildlands, hunting, trapping, and selling furs for what little money they wanted in order to buy items and ammunition. In books and films, Mountain Men are often portrayed as solitary hermits that lived alone and were grim, grimy, and grumpy all the time (Jeremiah Johnson is one example). In reality though, most often, Mountain Men traveled in groups or bands for safety and comradery.

Imagine getting injured in the vast wilderness all alone, you may be able to save yourself and you may not, but with a group, you are much more likely to enjoy life and actually live a long time. In addition to their group, Mountain Men would also trade extensively with Native American tribes, marry women from a tribe, and even occasionally join the tribe and live among them. They were not often lone wolves. In addition, hunting some large game such as bear, elk, and buffalo was far easier with many people. I can assure you, if you're hunting a bear or it charges you and you are forced to defend yourself, it's very unlikely that even the most powerful rifle will drop the bear instantaneously. Even if the bullet creates a fatal wound, the bear will usually live long enough to maul you, too. Successful bear hunting is far more attainable and appealing when there are many hunters who all fire together to increase their chances of getting some meat and coming out alive. Sorry, I know most of you all likely have never nor ever intended to hunt a grizzly bear, but I hope that relating this little anecdote about Mountain Men will help you see the merits of working as a team—it may mean your life in dark times ahead.

On a more positive note, also quite important to a successful friendship is humor. A stoic, dry, bleak-faced person may not be enjoyable to be around, whereas somebody with a strong sense of humor will be able to make people feel comfortable and relaxed around him/her and will be able to make hard times more tolerable by finding amusement in the little things. That's not to say you should be a clown all the time; somebody that can't take anything seriously is not a good candidate for a person to throw your cares on, to confide in, because such a goofy person wouldn't take your problems seriously. As with everything, it's a delicate balance. You should be able to make light of things, lighten the mood, and make life seem less overwhelming, while at the same time, you need to be able to listen attentively when your friend is in distress. Just listening is often the best way to help a distraught person. If you attempt to give them advice, only do so after listening until they're finished talking, then softly and gently give them useful advice—do not give advice that minimizes their problem.

By experience, I can tell you, and you've probably seen for yourself, that telling somebody to "calm down" is a terrible idea. Those words inevitably have the opposite effect on all but the mildest of people, it "riles them something terrible." Anger and severe perturbations will ensue if you take that wrong step, and seldom will any apologies soothe them. Also, when somebody confides in you about some problem or tragedy, I wouldn't recommend saying to them: "I understand." Their mental response is generally: "No, you don't understand; nobody can understand what I'm going through unless they've gone through it," and they likely find it difficult to conceal their annoyance at your untimely comment. Most of the time, just crying with them (if you are able), listening to them talk, and soothing them by putting your hand on their shoulder, holding their hand, or hugging them are the best options. In order to figure out the right response in each situation, try and imagine what it would feel like from their point of view, observe their body language, and listen to their tone of voice in order to feel for them (pity/sympathy), or better yet: feel with them (empathy). If you can accurately perceive how they're feeling, you will be more likely to respond appropriately. I know it may feel uncomfortable for you to comfort a grieving person, you may not know what to say, but that's not necessarily a bad thing: you might not have to say anything.

Of course, when it comes to touching somebody to comfort them, you'd probably only want to do that with friends and family you are very familiar with, though, if you come across as sincere and empathetic, even a complete stranger may sometimes appreciate it. Ultimately, it all comes down to your ability to read people's emotions, so practice that. For me, I'm not one to frequently make conversation with strangers, and certainly not hug a stranger! I'm far more comfortable and open with people than I used to be, but it's still a challenge—it's easy to stay within the confines of our "comfort zone." If you feel the same way, you're certainly not the only one. We would probably find it easier if we grew up in some remote and self-sufficient village or tribe where everybody knows each other from birth to death. I would be more comfortable in that situation, quite honestly, but few of us are, and if you were in that situation, you probably wouldn't be reading this book, now would you?

I suppose the key is to find like-minded, open, frank, honest, and unembarrassed people that easily show their feelings and happily accept them from others as well. That's easier said than done, though, right? I have found such people on occasion, but as I said, if what you currently have in life is not what you ultimately, really want, then you can't expect to find what you want and be able to stay in your comfort zone. If you could achieve your goals while living exactly as you are right now, then you would have already reached those goals by now. Sorry, but to follow your dreams, answer those deep and nagging questions within your soul, and fulfill the desires of your heart (the things you long for deep down without being aware of them), you are going to have to get out of your comfort zone. I repeat: escape your comfort zone. You are likely limiting yourself within a box of your own making, a prison of sorts. And you "can't escape a prison you don't know you're in."

In order to figure out if you've been living a lie, living an endless, redundant, repetitive, and futile rat race—you'll have to explore possibilities you never considered before. If you wish to seek the truth, you must at least once in your life question everything. Take nothing for granted. As a wise man once said, "It is the mark of an educated mind to be able to entertain a thought without accepting it." I was once told by a very wise and dear friend of mine: "The more one learns, the less one truly knows. Those who claim to know almost everything are clearly mistaken by the very fact they could believe such a thing. Our world, our reality is beyond all fathoming; those who reject the great mystery in it are misled." As a final quote for this little book, I shall take from an unlikely source, Star Wars, as the fictional character Obi-wan

Kenobi said, "Everything is true from a certain point of view." Would you humor me? Just think about that quote seriously for a bit...

This may be an overwhelming thought for you. You might think: "how can I tell what's true and what isn't, then?" The goal is not to find the truth, no one can find all truth, but to be constantly seeking truth, being content with the fact that we will never find it all, nor even be able to undeniably confirm any belief without a doubt. Our love for each other and our love for the truth, whatever that may be, is what binds us together, for to love is our only purpose in life.

Conclusion

I would like to sincerely thank you for making it through to the end of How to Make People Do What You Want. I hope it was informative and will provide you with some of the tools you need to achieve your goals, whatever they may be.

The next step is to apply the information. Reading alone is not enough to change your life, and one book alone is not enough to make you wise. We must keep searching if we would like to even begin to find the truth and gain freedom from it.

Therefore, in order to help you remember what you've read in this book, I'll give you a good summary of everything we discussed together. Do you remember how I told you in this book's introduction that I would spare you from having to read a long explanation of what you were about to read? Well, in my opinion, a long preview is useless, but a thorough review afterward helps cement what we learn in our minds (so information doesn't go in one ear and out the other). So please pardon me, but here is the part where I will go into a detailed review for you.

In Chapter 1: Develop Balanced Self-Confidence, we discussed how you can learn to think of yourself in a balanced way: neither think too much of yourself nor too little. How can you apply that? Serve others. If you live to help others, serve them, you cannot be insignificant because you will be an invaluable help to those around you, and you will be greatly appreciated. At the same time, because you are a servant, not a boss, you will not be corrupted by power, you will remain humble and self-sacrificing. Wealth and power tend to corrupt all but the most virtuous people, so do not wish to be rich and do not crave power. You will regret it later.

Your goal should be to have what you need and maybe a little extra to give to those around you. If you have big plans, you'll have big needs, but don't let your life become too complicated, or you may lose sight of what's important.

How can you serve others, though? Give spur-of-the-moment gifts to your friends and family; you don't need a holiday to do that. Help your neighbors out, especially the elderly and sickly, perhaps cooking for them, help them clean their house, help them grow their garden, or take them to appointments. You will have an inner joy from this as giving is better than getting.

Try and volunteer locally or perhaps even far away. Maybe pick up the litter along your road, help a local farmer (and hear some good stories and learn a thing or two), or whatever works for you. When opportunities come to do something new, something helpful, don't pass it up. It's rare that people regret doing good but often that they regret doing nothing at all.

If you have something good, you are obligated to share it with others, not just keep it to yourself. If you are feeling down, and you build others up with encouragement, surprisingly, you'll find yourself encouraged, too. We are not meant to live only for ourselves, so working together builds us all up.

Your lack of self-confidence may be from an old wound deep down from your childhood. The poison and festering infection in that wound may need drawing out. Drawing trauma back to the surface will be uncomfortable, but how much more uncomfortable would it be if you left it unresolved. Going to a therapist might help. And keep in mind that going to a therapist does not mean that you are insane. Really, we're all insane to an extent, it's just a matter of how much so. But you don't necessarily need outside help, you can try different forms of meditation to help you resolve your mental scars. Many people benefit from the Tapping technique, or EFT; perhaps you could do some research into these modalities.

For most people, though, too much confidence or too little confidence stems back to a disconnection from reality. They cannot see themselves as they really are. Engaging with hard manual labor outside is a good way to re-engage with the real world. The Amish have the right idea in that regard, hard work, they believe, keeps them grounded in practicality and keeps them down-to-earth. I've had some dealings with the Amish, and I've never yet met one that was unrealistic or haughty. In fact, the religion of the Amish is actually based very much upon humility. Their choice to remain separate from the modern world makes their communities reliant upon each other, and as such, they are held accountable for their actions. If an Amishman acts like a jerk, he will lose his reputation, and that will cause him trouble. If your boss acts like a jerk, you just have to grin and bear it—there's likely nobody who has the authority to set your boss straight. An Amish community must be interdependent because they truly do need each other. Our modern technological world gives each of us the illusion of independence, but we are very much reliant on others. Yes, you can work your job, make money, go to the store and buy what you want—nobody is helping you do these things. But at the same time, if it were not for modern industry: the factories producing your food, water, electricity, this book, and the items you use for your daily life, you would be sunk. So, in reality, our world is more interconnected than ever before, but unlike in the past, we are no longer interconnected as much with nature. Instead, we are interconnected with the industrial economy.

Many people, called homesteaders, gain pride by becoming self-sufficient in their needs so that they are not at the mercy of others to provide their very lifeline. This can give you confidence and a release from fear. If the world collapsed around you, which is not really so unlikely a scenario nowadays, you would be just fine. Maybe you'd have to be a little more careful about conserving your resources, but life would go on for you much as it did before. If you want to have the ultimate self-confidence, I urge you to rekindle your connection with nature.

Humility and a reasonable self-confidence are due to a recognition of your reality. Any imbalance in your life will affect your self-esteem in some negative way, so we do best to continually examine ourselves, observe and evaluate our actions, speech, and thoughts, along with taking the time to have solitude, peace, quiet, and stillness so as to have a clear mind and reassess our current trajectory in life. We cannot suppose that by treating life like a race that we'll be very happy.

On occasion, I've met people that are so busy, live so hectically, so over-occupied that they do not even understand the concept of patience or calm reflection. School Children nowadays are glued to their phones at every opportunity, and their use of technology is quite frivolous, just for pure entertainment. To talk to them about the beauty of nature would likely elicit a scoff from them, and they'd return to their familiar technology. Living in a virtual reality is a good way to, well, lose touch with reality. Oftentimes, kids will become so obsessed with devices that it will seem to them to be their whole life. As such, when somebody says something unkind to them on social media, it frequently causes them to fall into the bottomless pit of despair, get depressed, and sometimes, sadly, even commit suicide. The internet is their world, their life, and so a simple insult, rather than causing them to fight back, often leads them down a dark path. Our lives need to be based on more than one thing, one aspect, and we need to develop a thick skin that lets insults bounce off us without bothering us. That's easier said than done for somebody who wasn't raised that way, but doing hard manual labor will quickly change that. In the same way, as hard work causes us to develop calluses, which help our hands to be tougher and more resilient, in the same way, hard manual labor has the effect of making us more emotionally tough and resilient. If you live in the city, that'll be a challenge, but I encourage you to find some way of working hard, not just exercising, but actual, practical work. Like farming, gardening, digging, raising livestock, lifting heavy things, and so on. You may have to leave the city every once in a while to do such things, but you'll be better off for it.

In Chapter 2: Persuasive Techniques, First Impressions, and Body Language, we discussed how to present yourself in a way that makes you seem respectable. This applies to business situations, job interviews, casual conversations, and all interpersonal activities. You may be respectable or you just plain may not be, but if you give the clear impression that you are incompetent, weak, uninformed, awkward, or otherwise, whoever may be talking to you will not find you very appealing. That could cost you a job, your respect, your reputation, your romance, and your friendships. Good parents teach their children manners, common courtesy, politeness, decorum, and common sense from birth. But some parents, for whatever reason, may neglect to do so, perhaps their own parents never taught them manners, or perhaps their children just didn't absorb their parents' instruction. All I ask is this: if you have children or plan to have them, give them a good head start in life by teaching them manners. It's much harder to change your habits once they're established, so it's better to start early.

You may think that manners are silly and unnecessary, and I agree, many Victorian-like manners are absurd and baseless. And if you want to have a more relaxed family environment at home, by all means you can forgo them, but still show your kids how to act in public. Your kids may be very intelligent, very kind, very capable young people, but other people will never know it if your children seem boorish, crude, and rude. I am definitely a free thinker; I disagree with many, no, most of our modern traditions and customs, but I still know how to present myself as an appealing and mannerly person to strangers who do not understand my mentality. Once you and your children get to know people better, you can absolutely act more relaxed around them, it's only natural, but manners serve an important purpose in our society: to give the signal to others that they are respected. Don't withhold that respect from others; you and they will regret it.

The next step is to start meeting people, if this applies to you, in order to test your manners out. Your skills will increase the more you practice. I have found that the things I generally used to be nervous about: talking to strangers, job interviews, crowds, and whatnot—the anticipatory fear was worse than the actual experience. I'd always come away feeling comfortable and proud of myself; my fears were not well-founded. The things I fear, and the things you fear—they're not real, the fears are of your own making. At this point, all my fears have dissipated: I no longer fear death, nor pain, nor people, nor danger, nor being alone, nor starvation, nor failure, nor any potential misfortune. I enjoy life for what it is, and not what it is not. If I die, so be it, I prefer to live, but death is not something to be feared. The only thing I still fear is being trapped. The things you fear may well happen, so do your best to prevent them, but don't live in constant dread and desperation—if you do that, you won't be able to enjoy your current life either. Just learn to say: "So be it," to any misfortune that befalls you, "this too shall pass." We'll cross that bridge when we get there, as they say. So don't fear doing new things, in this case, meeting people.

Also, start treating your family and friends better right now. This will show you that you are capable of being more respectful, enjoy being so, and that others like it, too. It might seem odd at first to change your behavior with your family, especially if you've been habitually acting the same way for a long time, and other people might think you're acting odd, but don't misinterpret that—they do prefer respect, and so do you. Who doesn't want respect? But to get respect you have to give respect. Yes, you have to earn it, it is not a right but a privilege.

One of the foremost problems in our society is a sense of entitlement. Many people believe that they deserve special treatment, or they deserve a free handout, or they deserve respect or love without being respectful and loving to others. Such people will inevitably and eventually find that this is not how life works. This selfish, lazy, and brat-like attitude is symptomatic of the fundamental nature of our current Western society. We have things easy, really easy. You likely don't have to draw water from a well, or fill up a barrel from a spring and haul the water back to your house with a yoke on your shoulders. No, you twist a knob, and the water miraculously appears from the spigot. You probably don't have to hunt, garden, or gather wild plants; you may choose to do so as a hobby, but you don't have to because a quick trip to the grocery store and you'll have everything you want, whenever you want it. Life is too easy nowadays, and it makes people weak, makes them reliant upon others, and makes them feel entitled to receive things they never worked for. Think of your ancestors, though, just a hundred or so years ago, when those things were not options. When people only reaped from hard work. If you didn't work, for the most part, you didn't eat.

History shows us that easy, luxurious living makes weak people, weak people become decadent and demanding and have a sense of entitlement, these weak people create a weak society, and this weak society soon collapses into war, famine, and anarchy. It's happened again and again throughout history, is currently happening in certain countries around the world, and could soon happen in your country if something doesn't change quickly. We rely upon a system that is so fragile and so intricate that even a slight malfunction or natural disaster could spell the end of this age. If we rely upon this technology to supply everything we need, we will be utterly sunk if we lose it.

My point is not to go off on a rant about potential future disasters, but my point is that we can choose to continue being weak, but we may be forced to rapidly toughen up or die pretty soon. On the other hand, if we learn to be strong now, to get over our squeamishness, to learn how to take care of ourselves, to change our way of life to one that allows us to live more independently of the establishment—if we get tough now, we will be ready for whatever comes. And it doesn't have to be a worldwide catastrophe, it could be a loved one's death, losing your job, a divorce or break-up, a severe disease, an accident, or anything else. Why wait till then? If we toughen up and get calluses now, when things may be easy, we will be able to deal with worse hardships in the future.

Do not demand special treatment from others or even the government. You may call it your "rights," and that may be true, but truly examine yourself deeply for a moment, ask yourself:

"have I really earned these rights, do all people deserve them, are they really unalienable rights, or am I just asking for special treatment?" Many people ask for special treatment because they feel they were oppressed or held down, maybe so, but maybe they're just using that as an excuse to get a free handout. Where I grew up, I actually did meet plenty of people who were abused, mistreated, and oppressed, but I never heard them asking for free handouts and special treatment. They were tough people, strong people, hard-working people. They were ashamed to receive charity from anyone they thought was giving pity. These were the older people. On the other hand, our younger generations, whose parents often pampered and made excuses for them, they live in unprecedented luxury and ease and legal equality. But all that is not enough, their appetites are insatiable, greedy for handouts and praise, while getting rageful and bruised at the slightest put-down. These loud and boisterous voices that we hear speaking are not the voice of reason, reality, or even the majority. Those of you who belong to the pampered sort, don't suppose I mean to bother you, but consider taking this advice: turn that "belong to the pampered sort" into "belonged to that pampered sort." We can change, in fact, we will have to change. Times are getting no easier, and sooner or later, we're going to have to toughen up. If we wait till we have to, we'll make life harder for ourselves, whereas if we start getting tough now, we'll sail smoothly, or at least a good bit smoother than most people, through the raging, tempestuous seas of our coming hard times ahead. A big part of getting tough is actually earning what we get, not just believing we already deserve it. So start now: give respect to get respect.

In Chapter 3: Empathy, we went over various methods for you to learn how to feel for others. Sometimes this can be hard to learn. I know a man who is a good example: he truly believes he is a kind, balanced, yielding, normal, and reasonable person, but most everybody that knows him disagrees. Now don't get me wrong, he can be fun to be around on occasion, but staying with him for any extended period of time tends to be increasingly unpleasant. Now, mind you, he is oblivious to this.

My point is that even if you truly believe you are empathetic and kindhearted, you do well to carefully examine yourself. Now, living alone for a long time often makes people self-absorbed, not necessarily entirely selfish, but more focused on oneself than would be proper. Some people are just delusional, they live in a fantasy, they see themselves or a certain situation a certain way, and nothing you could say or do would change their mind. I suppose the problem is often when you give people power and authority over others. We've all seen corruption in politics, on all sides, and there's the old adage: "Power tends to corrupt, and absolute power corrupts absolutely." When we have no one to answer to, we can "get too big for our britches." For example, a father who rules over his family like a king, taking no input from his wife and treating his children in a dictatorial manner. Now, don't suppose a wife couldn't act the same way, in fact, nowadays, that seems even more frequent—matriarchy. But, on the other hand, imagine a primitive tribe such as our dearly beloved Native Americans in the past. Such tribes share everything, including power, so a parent or pair of parents do not have exclusive authority over their children or anybody else for that matter.

For example, a frequent societal system among various Native American tribes was the matrilineal system. Lineage and clan membership (similar in some respects to the Western concept of surnames) were based on a child's mother, instead of the father, the opposite of what is done in most modern societies. The children would be loved, cared for, and given advice by all the older people. The men had elders and war chiefs that would lead in battle based on their proven courage and prowess in previous battles. At the same, the men did not make all the decisions, for the war chiefs ultimately answered to the older women, the grandmothers. Do you see how that system is similar to a democratic government, with checks and balances? Whereas in many households nowadays, we often have a particular parent who is very dominant, and who makes most of the decisions independently. There is no higher authority in the family. This is one reason why there are more controversies in modern families, because all authority is placed in the hands of one or two people, as opposed to a whole tribe or village community.

My point is that when we have to work with others and others have to work with us, we are all better kept in our place. We are less likely to become selfish, and selfishness is the foremost enemy of empathy—how can you be keenly aware and concerned for others' welfare when your priority is only yourself?

The primary catalyst for change in our habits is contemplation. If we take the time to reflect on our day, ponder over the good and bad points, we'll see how to improve next time. Life is really just one continuous school, with plentiful lessons. If we ignore the lessons, then we cannot benefit from them and learn to improve ourselves in order to fulfill our purpose in life. If life keeps getting harder and harder, maybe we should consider that as a message to go in a different direction; don't stick to a plan just for the sake of it, be willing to adapt to curves along the way. Life does not have to be hard, if it is, there's something wrong and it should be our goal to figure out how to correct it and, in turn show others what we've found. We can learn the easy way or the hard way. We are often too thick-skulled to learn the easy way, so we'll experience hardships in life. The only good use for misfortunes is to learn from them and to do better the next time, but if we don't learn, then the hardship was all for nothing, it was entirely futile, it was to no avail, it did not benefit us whatsoever. If we sit in silent contemplation, much will occur to us that our active and manic minds will never reveal otherwise. If we see a way to improve our way of treating others, then imagine yourself doing it, play it out in your mind, practice it, then you'll do better when the real situation faces you. Learn to go into deep meditation so as to access our subconscious mind, to correct any imbalances that may be there, and reprogram our minds to think straight.

Another resource that you're currently making use of is books. Benefit from the skills and accumulated knowledge of others. I'm sorry to tell you, but I'm not your man for that! I just want to start you in a good direction. I do not claim to be the most experienced or wise of people, I'm not even close to the top of the list. Some extremely insightful and useful books I would recommend to you that you might not have heard of before are: How to Break the Habit of Being Yourself by Dr. Joe Dispenza and The Alchemist by Paulo Coelho, and plenty more besides. I highly recommend those two. Of course, religious texts, such as the Bible, are far more insightful, but they do take a lot of careful study, and not all of your studies will be especially interesting, so you have to be ready for that. If you are accustomed to immediate gratification of your desires, then careful study is not for you because it may take years to even begin to understand complicated subjects, let alone actively researching and contributing to them. Patience is a virtue, indeed.

Patience is also a major virtue with regards to empathy. Someone might unknowingly or even knowingly annoy you, and without patience, you'll be likely to lash out at them. Try to understand people's actions and attitudes from their point of view, do not impose your own mentality upon them. It would be foolish to suppose people all think the same way as us, we all have a different upbringing, background, heritage, culture, spirituality, lifestyle, and genetics for that matter.

To learn patience, try doing long projects, try building something, watching the wind in the treetops, practicing martial arts, learning an instrument, and so forth. Anything that would force you to slow down, relax, not expect immediate results, and learn to reach goals little by little rather than all at once. Life is often compared to a race, but it would be better to compare it to a journey. It's not a competition, it doesn't really matter how long you take to get where you're going, it's an experience, not a destination. The biggest part of improving yourself, in this case, becoming more empathetic, is to first understand there's room for improvement, that you could do better, and then to simply desire to improve and intend to do so. Intention alone, when strong and sustained consistently, is enough to lead us in the right direction. Now, an effort will be involved, and you will have to work for your goals, but the ferocious intention is a force to be reckoned with.

To accomplish anything, especially a change in personality, grit and courage are necessary. Grit to persevere and bust through the roadblocks. Courage to step outside the unknown, out of your comfort zone. Doing things that are uncomfortable can get you accustomed to bravery and grit. Wim Hof, if you have heard of him, is a perfect example of this. The man ran a marathon in the Arctic with nothing but shorts, and also frequently dunks himself in the coldest water possible. This has been proven to have a variety of benefits, including reduced inflammation, positive mood, energy, and mental clarity. You may not be ready to hop into an ice bath quite yet, but at least try this: after you've lathered up with suds in the shower, turn the water cold as it gets and thoroughly rinse off. There's no denying it—it's extremely uncomfortable and shocking, but it is absolutely invigorating afterward! Try keeping your breathing calm, slow, and relaxed; otherwise, you will begin to hyperventilate in shock. As long as you keep your breathing calm, it will be tolerable. Honestly, try it, it truly does make you feel good.

With all this, you might be wondering: "What does all this have to do with the subject of this book?" The answer: anything that helps you feel better, look better, have mental clarity, and toughens you will help you to overcome bad habits, start creating good ones, become more confident, more kind, more peaceful, more content, more sociable, more adventurous, more skilled, more curious, and just plain more balanced all around.

In Chapter 4: How to be Pleasant to be Around, we outlined how to appeal to people and become a universally attractive person. By attractive, I don't just mean your physical appearance, I know plenty of pretty people who I wouldn't trust to fry an egg. Appearance is part of it, I suppose, if you're plain ugly then it'll be hard for people to be attracted to you, even if you have a nice personality. It's possible to overlook appearance, and it's a wonderful thing to do so, but it can be hard to do at times. But take heart, my friend, there really are very few truly ugly people, and I highly doubt you are one of them, whatever you may think about yourself. We may not all be fit for a Greek marble statue, but then again not too many people are. It is far more important to focus on your inner beauty, the kind that really matters. A magnet might not be the prettiest thing you ever did see, but two magnets pointed in the right way towards each other will have an irresistible attraction.

In order to be that attractive, we need to learn to appeal to people. There are many kind, sincere, well-intentioned, and wise people I know that simply don't know how to present themselves to others. For example, you may be a hard-working and conscientious employee, but if you go to a job interview with your body covered in tattoos, your hair dyed strange colors and cut in an extreme and outlandish manner, you have various piercings, and you just have a general look of unkemptness and oddness— you probably can tell how your potential boss would react. You may be very respectful and carry on a good conversation, but your chosen appearance casts a shadow of doubt upon your character.

In the same way, you may look and dress fine for an occasion, but a lack of eye contact and manners could be a problem. Also, we may look respectable and speak well, but if we convey an attitude of over-confidence and inconsiderateness, that could also be a problem. This doesn't just apply to job interviews, in fact, most employers don't care how kindhearted their employees are as long as they do good work. This really applies better to familial relationships and friendships. If you don't know how to be appealing, you will make fewer friends, what friendships you do have will not be as close, and some friendships may be lost because of our unsavory personality. As I mentioned in chapter 4, having a good sense of humor is the primary quality that makes people approachable. You may be kind, but if you are stern, stoic, and unsmiling, people will not likely choose to befriend you. On the other hand, if you can take life a little lighter and see the humor in things, you will make people feel comfortable. That's not to say you should be a jokester either; then, when a serious subject arises, a friend would avoid confiding in you. It's a delicate balance. If you are a clown, try toning it down. Hey! That's a funny phrase to remember: "If you're a clown, tone it down." There's an example of humor, I just amused myself with that rhyme.

On the other hand, if you have trouble finding humor in life, follow this protocol. I'm not a trained doctor, but I identify as a doctor, so that makes me a doctor. As your humor doctor, I'm going to write you a prescription: read Tom Sawyer by Mark Twain. I guarantee you, my friend, you'll be busting open your sides from laughing, and if you don't learn a sense of humor from that, nothing will. If Tom Sawyer doesn't make you laugh, then you might have a serious health condition: Nolaughingitis, and you'll definitely need a better doctor than me, perhaps a psychologist. Putting my jokes aside, I sincerely hope that even if you already have a good sense of humor, Tom Sawyer will make it even better. It's hilarious, I assure you. Have you ever heard the saying: "Laughing is the best medicine"? It certainly is, just laughing, even when it's fake, makes you feel much better. It's what makes life most memorable and enjoyable.

Try it now, if there's nobody around to hear you, or even if there are people and you just don't care—try faking laughter. It works, it comes naturally, at least for me, just thinking about laughing makes me giggle, it's contagious like yawning. It's plenty of fun, it's a medicine that spreads to others, making your life more pleasant, and the same for those around you. Being kind, humble, and having a good sense of humor alone will make people excuse most mistakes of yours because you will be so pleasant to be around.

I know I said being pleasant to be around is not about physical beauty, but nonetheless, I'd like to give you a few simple tips on that subject while I'm on it. So, you would be wise to wash your face, smile, brush your teeth, wear clothes that look nice (if you're with city people; in the country, most folks don't care if you look like you just came out of a mudwallow), fix your hair decently, and so forth. Not to be rude, but if others smell objectionable odors only in your presence, they may feel the need to increase the distance between the two of you. If you have been chewing tobacco or eating chocolate, a good brushing might do the trick. Also, stand in a good posture, don't slump over. If you slouch, you'll look bored, uninterested, sad, tired, sickly, etc. I would recommend against strong perfumes and colognes because they can be overpowering and distracting. I would also recommend against wearing jeans that look like they've been mauled by a panther (ripped jeans). My work jeans get ripped from hard work, but then I sew them back together. Of course, everybody is entitled to their own opinion, but in my opinion, it seems silly to purposefully buy jeans that are ruined before you even use them; leave it to modern fashion to convince people to wear and do odd things! Heavy makeup is also distracting and extreme-looking. Everything in moderation.

Also, if you like people, don't be afraid to show it. This is not just about romantic interest, it also applies equally to friends, young or old. If you feel you've found a "kindred-spirit," then seek to further that friendship. Old people generally enjoy the company of young people, but many young people only want to be around those of their own age. I understand that, it's only natural that we should be drawn to people at a similar stage in life. And, of course, if you want to go backpacking in the wilderness, old granny may not be the companion you're looking for. But I believe that each of us is enriched by a variety of companions. Those of the other sex, younger folks, older folks, people of all backgrounds and upbringings. Now, I won't lie, being from the country myself, I can tolerate the company of city people only so long before I yearn to be among my own kind again. But, every once in a while, it may be nice to shake things up a bit, to meet strange people. It's only by chance/coincidence, destiny/fate, or searching/scouring that you'll find the right people for you; or maybe you already have them right now, right at home, you've known them since birth—your family.

Oftentimes we have to lose something before you can truly appreciate it. You may have to leave your family, your homeland, your culture, maybe even your beliefs for a while, in order to realize that the treasure you sought was at home all along. Or maybe you were born for a different way of life, it's up to you to find out. Don't content yourself with reading books and watching movies about adventure, do it yourself! Go on your own journey.

In Europe, it is common practice for young people just-graduated, to go on an adventure before they commit to college or a job, to satisfy that fundamental urge to wander freely—it is called a Gap Year. In America, unfortunately, this is very uncommon. Most graduates immediately go on to a job, college, or just do nothing and mooch off their parents. What if we made a Gap Year a tradition in America? Wouldn't that enrich our young people? In Europe, the working hours are lower, and vacation days are more numerous. In America, we, on average, work longer than the average Medieval serf, and I am serious about this.

How long will you spend your life not doing the things you love, doing the same thing over and over and over again, running the rat race round and round the hamster wheel day after day? How long will you keep wishing it isn't Monday, then wish it was the weekend, then wish it was a vacation, then wish you were retired? Let me give you the answer to those questions, let me tell you what'll happen if you don't know yet: pretty soon, you'll wish your whole life away. It is strange how it's generally older folks that end up living their dreams (albeit probably not as they imagined because they are not quite as spry as they used to be), while the young, wild, adventurous kids force themselves to study and labor. There is still plenty of mystery and adventure left in the world, it's up to you to find it. Once again, I'll recommend to you The Alchemist by Paulo Coelho because it does a perfect, wonderfully entertaining, enlightening job of showing what I just said. It is an allegorical tale about a young Spanish shepherd boy from Andalusia who has a dream about a treasure, which leads him on a marvelous journey across the Sahara desert of North Africa. It is a wonderful book, and to be honest, far better than this one!

I was once asked in school: "What is freedom?" Everybody sees freedom as something a little different. Sometimes our ideas about freedom might interfere with the freedoms of others. Consider this: to you, what is freedom? It might take a little while to figure it out and find the right words to express it. To me, put simply, freedom is the ability to reach my full potential in life, to accomplish my purpose in life, to be a seeker of truth. That doesn't interfere with the freedoms of others, now, does it? In fact, I hope to use my freedom to help many people.

If you know what freedom is to you, you will know whether or not you are achieving that freedom. You may realize that, according to your definition of freedom, you may not currently be free, you might be in prison. If so, then figure out how to become free. I say this so that you will be content and at peace with yourself, with life, and with others. If you are trapped in a cage, like a poor bird, yearning to fly free, you will beat your wings against the metal bars until they're bloody, peck the cage until your beak breaks. If you do that, you will be unhappy and everyone around you will sense it and suffer; eventually, they will grow tired of being with a person who lashes out at them because you are not free and yearn to be free.

To have good friends, not "friends" that you make with the tap of a button on social media, nor just acquaintances, nor just even people you "hang out" with, no, I want you to have lifelong companions that stand by you through thick and thin. Have you ever heard the country song, Find Out Who Your Friends Are? In it, the lyrics say: "Get yourself in a bind...you find out who your friends are, somebody's gonna drop everything, run out and crank up their car, hit the gas, get there fast, never stop to think 'what's in it for me' or 'it's way too far,' they just show on up, with a big old heart." I pray that such friends may be your companions through life, and that you likewise help them through the trials and tribulations of life, and that you have or find your foremost friend on earth, your spouse.

In Chapter 5: Understanding Psychology, we dove into the subject of how humans think, how you and I think, how our ways of thinking affect our lives, and what we can do to change our thinking to go in a better direction. As usual, the next step is to put it to practice.

The foremost thing I want you to get out of this chapter, and this whole book, is that we are all interconnected, that we do better together. The best way to make life easy, make friends, be self-sufficient, and be connected with nature is to make a community of like-minded people. You don't have to join some commune or start one, in your own neighborhood you could start this on a small scale. Help your neighbors out, not asking for anything in return. Do errands, mow the grass, shovel the snow, and whatnot.

If you start doing "good turns" without being paid, your neighbors will likewise feel the need to help you out when you need them. Paying people for a service settles the debt, so that no one needs to feel beholden or indebted to another person. But if we would create a system of helping each other without expectation of reward, recompense, or payment, we will create a better neighborhood and better people therein. If you have some junk, "one man's junk is another man's treasure," ask around and see who needs it or put it outside with a "Free" sign on it. Share your tools with your neighbors, give them gifts, talk to them, have them over for dinner or a game of some sort, have a block party, have a community garden, and the list of endless possibilities goes on and on.

Extend your community beyond the bounds of mankind. Get to know the forest around your place, get to know the plants and animals. I know each and every tree where I grew up, every hummingbird, every lizard, every frog, and every hill and hole. Learn the wild plants in your area, wherever you may be, I guarantee you that you have a veritable garden growing wild somewhere nearby. Knowing the plants gives you plenty of good things to eat for free, it immerses you in your landscape, and makes you happier. Here are a few resources: get the book Peterson Field Guide to Edible Wild Plants, if you have a device, download the app Plantnet, which will help you accurately identify your local plants with more certainty than a book can. Go on local foraging walks (do some research to find one in your area), check out the outdoorsman, Rob Greenfield's site https://www.robgreenfield.org/findaforager/ to find a good forager near you. Mr. Greenfield also has a YouTube channel called by his name, which I encourage you to check out for its numerous useful tips.

Of course, many people would not like this, but I just want to give you some pointers. If you want, learn how to hunt and fish, if you don't already know how. With regards to fishing, figure out what would work best in your area, whether it be surf fishing, creek fishing, lake fishing, river fishing, fly fishing, or whatever else. Learn the techniques and get the appropriate equipment. With regards to hunting, find a suitable firearm, or if you would prefer, a bow or crossbow. Learn how to use it safely, take a hunter's education course, get a license, and find some good spots in your area. I understand you may despise the thought of killing an animal, but it could give you a way of getting cheap food when things get too expensive, especially if you don't yet have a farm. Also, relying on nature as your source of livelihood, even if only in a small way (just for fun), it makes you feel more whole and fulfilled.

Here's a good example of neighborliness: one of my relatives, who lives in a Latino neighborhood, would see goats wandering around and grazing on people's yards. What did he do? Call animal control? Call the sheriff? Some of my neighbors have unfortunately done that. No, he thought nothing of it, he just enjoyed watching them. His neighbors, who at the time didn't know him, invited him to a block party. They slaughtered one of their goats, made all kinds of Mexican cuisine, and played mariachi music. By the end of it, he was good friends with all his neighbors. If you have a problem with what your neighbors are doing, don't go to the police, go to them! Honestly, that is the act of a coward to hide inside the house and call the authorities on your own neighbor. But, nowadays, in this modern world, being a neighbor doesn't really mean much. Most people have never met them, or even if they have met them they hardly know them. People love to be independent and private, so be it, that's their choice. Life is easier and happier with a broad community to support you, "many hands make the load light."

Create a close-knit tribe, and don't limit it only to your blood relatives. I once saw a doormat that said: "Friends are your chosen family." Please do not keep friends at arms' length, don't hold them back, don't shut them out. Right now, it seems to be a choice to be neighborly or not, but in the future, we may be forced to rely on each other. When times get hard, which may not be as far off as you think, the people you'll need will not be your family across the country, across the state, or even across the town— they'll be your neighbors across the street. Grow a good relationship with them now to make it easier when things get hard. Out West in the USA, during the frontier period, gunslingers and "hired guns" would say: "there's only the fast and the dead." No in-betweens. If you do not know, this is referring to a gunman's quickness to the draw.

We may not be engaging in duels in the future, but we probably will be engaging in a scramble to survive. We see it every time a hurricane comes: people rush to the stores, empty the shelves, and stock up; same thing happens when there's some kind of shortage, people will literally fight each other to get a tank of gas. Most people's "civilized" nature disappears when civilization disappears; and what ensues? Violence, brutality, injustice, barbarism, selfishness, destruction, sickness, and death. I want you to have the advantage when that dreaded day comes, I want you to draw your gun even before the gunfight, I want you to survive. This is not just grim theorization, our society, inch by inch, little by little, descends into disaster. Our modern, technological lifestyle is inherently negative and destructive to our minds, bodies, and the land. It will inevitably catch up to us at some point, in one way or another. It may not be in your lifetime, but then, prepare your children for whatever comes, make them strong, tough, kind, and good. Teach them honesty, give them a community wherein to play outside and make friends, to dig holes, and climb trees. Give them a future and a hope. May it not be, that our desperation to make money and move up the ladder—may it not be that these things deprive our children from their inheritance: a world of plentiful nature and freedom.

To be completely honest, this all seems overly complicated to me, I wish the world was simpler. In a simpler world, you wouldn't have to spend your hard-earned money on a book about making friends, you'd just have friends! But this is a choice, we can choose to simplify our lives. All I ask of you is that you work hard to find a way of creating a healthy, wholesome, natural, and harmonious environment for yourself, your family, and those around you who you are able to help. My goal is for you to not need this book. My goal is for you to burn this confounded book! When you're ready, just embrace your destruction tendencies and set this book afire. You won't need it any more.

As a parting request before you put down this book, if you found this book useful, then we would be much obliged if you would write a review on Amazon and share it with your friends and family to help them on their journey as well. I hope I helped you in some little way. There's much more to do out there, plenty of mystery, frontier, and adventure left for the taking—chase after it!

In all that you do, I wish you only the very best.